W9-AQC-891

## ALSO BY ARNOLD SCHWARZENEGGER

*Total Recall:*
*My Unbelievably True Life Story*
(with Peter Petre)

*Terminator Vault:*
*The Complete Story Behind the Making of*
*The Terminator and Terminator 2:*
*Judgment Day* (foreword)

*Arnold's Fitness for Kids*
(with Charles Gaines)

*Encyclopedia of Modern Bodybuilding*
(with Bill Dobbins)

*Arnold's Bodybuilding for Men*
(with Bill Dobbins)

*The Education of a Bodybuilder*
(with Douglas Kent Hall)

# ARNOLD SCHWARZENEGGER

# BE USEFUL

## SEVEN TOOLS FOR LIFE

*Penguin Press   New York   2023*

PENGUIN PRESS
An imprint of Penguin Random House LLC
penguinrandomhouse.com

Copyright © 2023 by Fitness Publications, Inc.
Penguin Random House supports copyright. Copyright fuels creativity,
encourages diverse voices, promotes free speech, and creates a vibrant culture.
Thank you for buying an authorized edition of this book and for complying
with copyright laws by not reproducing, scanning, or distributing any part
of it in any form without permission. You are supporting writers and allowing
Penguin Random House to continue to publish books for every reader.

LIBRARY OF CONGRESS CATALOGING-IN-PUBLICATION DATA

Names: Schwarzenegger, Arnold, author.
Title: Be useful : seven tools for life / Arnold Schwarzenegger.
Description: New York : Penguin Press, 2023.
Identifiers: LCCN 2023019948 (print) | LCCN 2023019949 (ebook) |
    ISBN 9780593655955 (hardcover) | ISBN 9780593656716
    (international edition) | ISBN 9780593655962 (ebook)
Subjects: LCSH: Success. | Self-actualization (Psychology) |
    Resilience (Personality trait)
Classification: LCC BF637.S8 S375 2023 (print) |
    LCC BF637.S8 (ebook) | DDC 158.1—dc23/eng/20230601
LC record available at https://lccn.loc.gov/2023019948
LC ebook record available at https://lccn.loc.gov/2023019949

Printed in the United States of America
1st Printing

LSCH

Book design by Daniel Lagin

# CONTENTS

# INTRODUCTION

A few months after I left the governor's office in 2011, my world came crashing down around me.

It's not like things had been going so great in the years before that. After winning a landslide reelection with 57 percent of the vote in 2006, then passing environmental policies that inspired the world and making the biggest infrastructure investment in California history—one that will serve California's drivers, students, and farmers long after I'm gone—my final two and a half years in the Capitol, which I spent in the thick of the global financial crisis, felt like being stuck in a clothes dryer with a load of bricks. It was nothing but beating after beating from every direction.

In 2008, when the crash hit, it was as if one day people

were starting to lose their homes, and the next day we were in the biggest recession since the Great Depression, all because a bunch of greedy bankers brought the world's financial system to its knees. One day California was celebrating a record budget windfall that allowed me to set up rainy-day funds. The next day the fact that California's budget was too tied to Wall Street left us with a $20 billion shortfall and dragged us nearly into insolvency. I spent so many late nights locked in a room with the leaders of both parties in the legislature, trying to pull us back from the brink, that it felt like the state might legally recognize us as domestic partners.

But the people didn't want to hear any of that. They just knew that we'd cut their services while we raised their taxes. You can explain that governors don't have control over a global financial disaster—but the truth is, you get credit when the economy's on the way up even though you have very little to do with it, so it's only fair that you get the blame on the way down. It just doesn't feel good.

Don't get me wrong. We had some wins. We blew up the system that had given political parties virtual veto power over the best interests of the people and turned our politicians into do-nothing losers. We beat the oil companies trying to undo our environmental progress and moved forward even more aggressively—we blanketed the state in solar power and other renewables and made historic investments to lead the world in clean technology.

But I learned in those last years of the 2000s that you can pass some of the most groundbreaking, cutting-edge policies that state government has ever seen and you'll still feel like a total failure when a voter asks why you can't keep them in their home, or a parent asks why you cut their kid's school budget, or workers ask why they've been laid off.

This wasn't my only experience with public failure, obviously. I had dramatic losses in my bodybuilding career, I had movies that went in the toilet, and this wasn't the first time I'd watched my approval ratings fall like the Dow Jones Industrial Average.

But I wasn't even close to rock bottom.

And it wasn't the recession that brought my world crashing down.

I did that to myself.

I blew up my family. No failure has ever felt worse than that.

I won't be rehashing that story here. I've told it before in other places, and other places have told it multiple times. All of you know the story. If you don't, you've heard of Google, and you know how to find it. I've hurt my family enough, and it's been a long road to repair those relationships; I will not turn them into fodder for the gossip machine.

What I will say is that by the end of that year, I had found myself in a place that was both familiar and foreign. I was at the bottom. I'd been here before. But this time, I was face down in the mud, in a dark hole, and I had to decide whether it was worth it to clean myself up and start the slow climb out, or to just give up.

The movie projects I'd been working on since I left the Capitol went up in smoke. The cartoon loosely based on my life I was so excited about? Bye-bye. The media wrote me off—my story would be over after three acts: Bodybuilder, Actor, Governor. Everybody loves a story that ends in tragedy, especially when it is the mighty who have fallen.

If you've ever read anything about me, though, you probably already know that I didn't give up. In fact, I relish the challenge of having to climb back up. It's the struggle that makes success, when you achieve it, taste so sweet.

My fourth act has been an amalgamation of all three

previous acts, combined to make me as useful as I can, with a little something else added in that I didn't expect. I continue my bodybuilding and fitness crusade with a daily fitness email to hundreds of thousands of hungry people and my Arnold Sports Festivals all over the world. My policy work goes on at After-School All-Stars, where we serve one hundred thousand kids in forty cities across the nation; at the USC Schwarzenegger Institute for State and Global Policy, where we advocate for our political reforms all over the United States; and at the Schwarzenegger Climate Initiative, where we sell our environmental policies all over the world. And my entertainment career? That pays for it all. This time, after climbing out of the Hollywood wilderness doing movie after movie, I returned with a television series, which is a new creative medium for me that I've enjoyed enormously trying to master.

I knew I'd continue all those careers. Like I always tell you, I'll be back. But what I never expected was that, as a by-product of all this failure and redemption and reinvention, I'd become a self-help guy.

Suddenly, people were paying me as much as former presidents to show up and give motivational speeches to their clients and their workforces. Other people were taking the videos of those speeches, putting them on You-Tube and on social media, and they were going viral. Then my own social media channels started to grow, because anytime I used them to share my wisdom about urgent matters of the day or to offer a calm voice amid the chaos, those videos went even more viral.

People really seemed to benefit from learning from me, the same way I benefited early in my career from reading about and meeting my idols, many of whom you will hear about in this book. So I leaned into that. I started spreading more and more positivity out in the world. And the more I spoke, the more people came up to me in the gym to tell me that I'd gotten them through a dark time. Cancer survivors, people who had lost their jobs, people transitioning into the next phase of their career. I heard from men and women, boys and girls, high school kids and retirees, rich people, poor people, every color, creed, and orientation in the rainbow of humanity.

It was fantastic. It was also surprising. I wasn't sure why this was happening. So I did what I always do when I want to understand something. I stopped and analyzed the situation. What I noticed when I took a step back was that there was so much negativity and pessimism and

self-pity out in the world. I also noticed that a lot of people were really miserable, despite the fact that experts
keep telling us that things have never been better in the
history of human civilization. There has never been less
war, less disease, less poverty, less oppression than right
now. This is what the data shows. It's objectively true.

But there is another set of data. A more subjective set
that is harder to measure but that we can all see and hear
when we watch the news, or listen to talk radio, or scroll
on social media. So many people talk about feeling irrelevant or invisible or hopeless. Young girls and women talk
about not being good enough or pretty enough. Young
men talk about being worthless or powerless. Incidents
of suicide and rates of addiction are on the rise.

In the wake of the COVID-19 pandemic, in particular, we are experiencing an epidemic of these emotions
across virtually every segment of our society. Depression
and anxiety have increased 25 percent worldwide since
2020. In a study by the Boston University School of
Public Health published in September 2020, researchers discovered that the prevalence of depression among
US adults had *tripled* between 2018 and the spring of
2020, just a few months into the lockdowns. Whereas

before, 75 percent of American adults reported feeling no symptoms of depression, by April 2020 that number had dropped to under 50 percent. That's a huge swing!

But the problem goes beyond COVID-19, because there are groups out there—entire institutions and industries, if we're being honest about it—that are taking advantage of people's misery and selling them nonsense, making them angrier, feeding them lies, and inflaming their grievances. All for profit and political gain. These forces are incentivized to keep people miserable and helpless, and to obscure how simple it should be for them to engage with the tools of usefulness and self-sufficiency that are the primary weapons in the fight against unhappiness and apathy.

That, I think, is why so many millions of people all over the world have flocked to podcasts and Substacks and newsletters like mine in search of answers that make sense to them. Things have gotten so bad out there in the culture that they are seeking out someone they can trust, someone who refuses to play the bullshit games, someone who tries to be ruthlessly positive when everyone else is being relentlessly negative.

Those are the people I was bumping into at the gym every single day. And I felt a kinship with them because they were expressing a lot of the same emotions I felt after I left office in 2011 and things fell apart. I also noticed that when I offered them advice and encouragement, when I tried to inspire and reassure them and pump them up, I was pulling from a very familiar tool kit.

It was the tool kit that I'd developed over the course of sixty years and followed successfully on my journey through the previous three acts of my life. It was the very same one I reached for more than a decade ago now, when I hit bottom and decided to dig myself out of the hole. This tool kit is not revolutionary. If anything, it's timeless. These tools have always worked. They always will work. I think of them like elements of a blueprint or a road map to a happy, successful, useful life—whatever that means for you.

They involve knowing where you want to go and how you're going to get there, as well as having the willingness to do the work and the ability to communicate to the people you care about that the journey you want to bring them on is worth the effort. They include the capacity to shift gears when the journey hits a roadblock, and the ability to keep an open mind and learn from your surroundings to find new ways through. And most important of all, once you get where you're trying to go, they demand that you acknowledge all the help you had along the way and that you give back accordingly.

This book is called *Be Useful* because that is the best piece of advice my father ever gave me. It has stuck in my brain and never left, and my hope is that the advice I am offering you in the pages to follow will do the same thing. Being useful was also the motivating force behind all my decisions, and the organizing force around the tools I used to make them. Being a bodybuilding champion, being a millionaire leading man, being a public servant—those were my goals, but they were not what motivated me.

For a number of years, my father didn't agree with my version of what it means to be useful, and I might not agree with your version, when it comes down to it. But that is not the purpose of good advice. It's not to tell you what to build, it's to show you how to build and why it matters. My father passed away at the same age I was when I brought my world crashing down on me. I never had the chance to ask him what I should do, but I have a good idea what he would tell me: "Be useful, Arnold."

I wrote this book to honor those words and pay forward his advice. I wrote it in appreciation for the years I've had that he didn't, which I've used to make amends, to climb back from the bottom, and to build the fourth act of my life. I wrote this book because I believe that anyone can benefit from the tools I've used through every phase of my life, and that all of us need a reliable road map for the kind of life we've always wanted to live.

But most of all, I wrote it because everybody needs to be useful.

# BE USEFUL

**CHAPTER 1**

# HAVE A CLEAR VISION

So many of our best people are lost.

So many of the good ones don't know what they're doing with their lives. They're unhealthy. They're unhappy. Seventy percent of them hate their jobs. Their relationships are unrewarding. They don't smile. They don't laugh. They have no energy. They feel useless. They feel helpless, as if life were pushing them down a road to nowhere.

If you know what to look for, you will see these people everywhere. Maybe even when you look in the mirror. It's OK. You're not broken. Neither are they. This is just what happens when you don't have a clear vision for your life, and you've taken either whatever you can get or whatever you thought you deserved.

We can fix that. Because everything good, all great change, starts with a clear vision.

Vision is the most important thing. Vision is purpose and meaning. To have a clear vision is to have a picture of what you want your life to look like and a plan for how to get there. The people who feel most lost have neither of those. They don't have the picture or the plan. They look in the mirror and they wonder, "How the hell did I get here?" but they don't know. They've made so many decisions and taken so many actions that have landed them in this place, and yet they have no idea what any of them were. They'll even argue with you: "I hate this, why would I have *chosen* it?" Except no one forced that ring on their finger or put that second cheeseburger in their hands. No one made them take that dead-end job. No one made them skip class, or miss workouts, or stop going to church. No one made them stay up late every night playing video games instead of getting eight hours of sleep. No one made them drink that last beer or spend their last dollar.

Yet they fully believe what they're saying. And I believe they believe it. They feel as if life just sort of happened to them. They really think they had no choice in what became of their lives.

And you know what? They're partly right.

None of us has a choice about where we come from. I grew up in a small village in Austria at the beginning of the Cold War. My mother was very loving. My father was strict, and he could be physically abusive, but I loved him very much. It was complicated. I'm sure your story is complicated too. I bet growing up was more difficult than the people around you think it was. We can't change those stories, but we can choose where we go from there.

There are reasons and explanations for all the things that have happened to us up to this point, good and bad. But for the most part, it wasn't because we didn't have a choice. We always have a choice. What we don't always have, unless we create it, is something to measure our choices against.

That is what a clear vision gives you: a way to decipher whether a decision is good or bad for you, based on whether it gets you closer or further away from where you want your life to go. Does the picture you have in your mind of your ideal future get blurrier or sharper because of this thing you're about to do?

The happiest and most successful people in the world do everything in their power to avoid bad decisions that confuse matters and drag them away from their goals. Instead, they focus on making choices that bring clarity to their vision and bring them closer to achieving it. It doesn't matter if they're considering a small thing or a huge thing, the decision-making process is always the same.

The only difference between them and us, between me and you, between any two people, is the clarity of the picture we have for our future, the strength of our plan to get there, and whether or not we have accepted that the choice to make that vision a reality is ours and ours alone.

So how do we do that? How do we create a clear vision from scratch? I think there are two ways to do it. You can start small and build out until a big, clear picture reveals itself to you. Or you can start very broad and then, like the lens on a camera, zoom in until a clear picture snaps into focus. That's how it was for me.

## START BROAD AND ZOOM IN

The earliest vision I had for my life was very broad. It was of America. Nothing more specific than that. I was ten years old. I'd just started school in Graz, the big city just east of where I grew up. It seemed like everywhere I turned in those days I was seeing the most amazing things about America. In my school lessons, on magazine covers, in newsreels that played before shows at the movie house.

There were pictures of the Golden Gate Bridge and those Cadillacs with the big tail fins driving down massive six-lane highways. I watched movies made in Hollywood and rock 'n' roll stars on talk shows filmed in New York. I saw the Chrysler Building and the Empire State Building, which made the tallest building in Austria look like a toolshed. I saw streets lined with palm trees and beautiful girls on Muscle Beach.

It was America in surround sound. Everything was big and bright. For an impressionable kid like me, those images were like Viagra for dreams. They should have come with a warning, too, because the visions of life in America they aroused did *not* go away after four hours.

I knew: this is where I belong.

Doing what? I had no clue. Like I said, it was a broad vision. The picture was very fuzzy. I was young. What did I know? What I would learn, though, is that some of the strongest visions emerge like this. From our obsessions when we're young, before our opinions about them have been affected by other people's judgments of them. Talking about what to do when you're dissatisfied with your life, the famous big wave surfer Garrett McNamara once said that you should "go back to when you were three, figure out what you loved doing, figure out how to make that your life, then make the road map and follow it." He was describing the process for creating a vision, and I think he's absolutely correct. It's obviously not that easy, but it is that simple, and it can begin by looking back in time and thinking very broadly about the things you used to love. Your obsessions are a clue to your earliest vision for yourself, if only you had paid attention to them in the beginning.

Look at someone like Tiger Woods showing off his putting skills on *The Mike Douglas Show* when he was only two years old. Or the Williams sisters. A lot of people don't know this, but their father, Richard, exposed all five of his kids to tennis when they were young, and they all had talent. But it was only Venus and Serena who showed passion for the sport. *Obsession.* And so tennis became the framework for how they grew up and how they saw themselves.

It was the same for Steven Spielberg. He wasn't a big movie fan when he was a boy. He loved TV. Then one year his dad got a little 8mm home movie camera for Father's

Day to record their family road trips, and Steven started to mess around with it. Around the same age I was when I was first learning about America, Steven discovered moviemaking. He made his first movie when he was twelve years old. He made one to earn a merit badge for photography in the Boy Scouts when he was thirteen. He even took the camera with him on Boy Scout trips. For Steven, who had just moved with his family all the way across the country from New Jersey to Arizona, moviemaking gave him his first bit of direction.

It wasn't moving to Hollywood. It wasn't winning an Oscar for Best Picture or Best Director. It wasn't being rich and famous or working with glamorous movie stars. Those more specific ambitions would all come later. In the beginning his vision was simply to make movies. It was big and broad, like it was for Tiger (golf), Venus and Serena (tennis), and me (America).

This is perfectly normal. For most of us, it's necessary. Anything more detailed gets too complicated too quickly, and you get ahead of yourself. You start missing important steps on the road map. Having a broad vision gives you an easy, more accessible place to start from when it comes to figuring out where and how to zoom in.

That doesn't mean you get narrower with your vision,

just more specific. The picture gets sharper. It's like zooming in on a map of the world when you're trying to build an itinerary for a trip. The world is made up of continents. Inside continents are countries, inside countries are states or provinces, inside those are counties, and inside those are cities and towns. And the thing is, you can keep going like this. Inside towns are neighborhoods, inside neighborhoods are blocks. Blocks are stitched together by streets. If you're a tourist and you just want to see the world, you can hop from country to country or city to city and it doesn't matter. You don't have to pay close attention. But if you really want to know a place and get the absolute most out of your experience, if you might even want to call that place home someday, well then, you better hit the streets, talk to locals, explore every back alley, learn the customs, and try new things. That is when the itinerary you're trying to create—or the plan you're trying to build to achieve your vision—really starts to take shape.

My plan took shape around bodybuilding, after the first clear picture of my future snapped into focus. I was a teenager and I saw the current Mr. Universe, the great Reg Park, on the cover of one of Joe Weider's muscle magazines. I'd just watched him play Hercules in *Hercules and the Captive Women* that summer. The article described how, as a poor kid from a working-class town in England, Reg discovered bodybuilding, then made the transition into acting after winning the Mr. Universe competition. I immediately saw it: that was my path to America.

For you, the path will be different; so will the destination. Maybe it involves a career choice and a change in scenery. Maybe it involves a hobby that you want to turn into a lifestyle or a cause that you want to make your life's mission. There really isn't a wrong answer as long as it sharpens the focus of your vision and makes the steps you need to take to achieve it more clear-cut.

Still, this part can be very difficult for people, even those with the broadest of visions. When I go to the gym these days, for example, I will sometimes see a person wandering around, bouncing randomly from machine to machine like a Ping-Pong ball, and it's clear they have no plan at all for their workout. I'll go up to this person, and we'll have a conversation. I've done this many times, and it always goes the same way.

"What's your goal coming into the gym?" I'll ask them.

"To get in shape," is what they'll usually say.

"Yes, great, fantastic, but get in shape for what?" I will say. It's an important question, because not all forms of "in shape" are created equal. Being in bodybuilder shape isn't going to help you if you're a rock climber. If anything, it's going to hurt you having to carry around all that extra mass. In the same way, being in shape like a long-distance runner is useless if you're a wrestler, where you need both raw strength and explosive quickness.

They'll pause, then they'll stammer, searching for an answer that they think I want to hear. But I stay silent, I don't let them off the hook. Eventually, most of them give me an honest answer.

"My doctor said I need to lose twenty pounds and get my blood pressure under control."

"I just want to look good at the beach."

"I have young kids and want to be able to chase them around and wrestle with them."

These are all great answers. I can work with each of them. Zooming in like that gives their vision some specific direction, which will help them focus on the exercises that are best for achieving that goal.

Bodybuilding is all about zooming in. Not just on the

specifics of what you want to achieve as a bodybuilder, but also on the steps you need to take in the gym to get there. When I got to America as a twenty-one-year-old in the fall of 1968 and I landed in Venice Beach to train at Gold's Gym under the great Joe Weider, I'd already won a number of titles, including Mr. Universe earlier that year, in my professional debut. Those titles were steps on the path that brought me to Joe's attention, which ultimately brought me to America. But they were not the final steps. Joe didn't pay for me to come to America because I'd already become a champion. He was investing in me because he thought I could be *more* than a champion. I was still very young by bodybuilding standards. I also had an incredible hunger to work hard and an insane desire to be great. Joe saw all these things in me and thought I had a real shot to be the greatest bodybuilder in the world, maybe even of all time. And he was going to help me zoom in even closer to really figure out what it takes to become the greatest ever.

I was in America, I was Mr. Universe, and the work was just beginning.

## CREATE SPACE AND TIME

Of course, not everyone starts to develop an idea of what they want to do with their life by the time they're fifteen years old, like I did. I was fortunate. I grew up in a small village with dirt roads, in a house with no running water or indoor plumbing. I had nothing but time and space to daydream and let my imagination run wild. I was a blank slate. Anything and everything could make an impression on me. And it did.

Pictures of America. Playing gladiators in the park with my friends. Reading a news article for school about a record-breaking powerlifter. Finding out that one of my friends knew Mr. Austria, Kurt Marnul, and that he trained right there in Graz. Watching *Hercules and the Captive Women* and learning that Hercules was played by Mr. Universe, and that the actor who played Hercules before him, Steve Reeves, was also Mr. Universe. Then stumbling upon one of Joe Weider's muscle magazines and seeing Reg on the cover, and learning that he was from a small working-class town just like me.

All of these things were moments of inspiration that

imprinted on me. They combined not just to create the earliest vision that I had, but then to clarify and sharpen it, which would give me something specific to work toward for the next twenty years.

For a lot of people, finding that kind of vision is a long-term discovery process that takes years, if not decades. Some never get there. They live with no vision. Not even memories of an early obsession when they were young that could become a vision now as an adult. Those memories and the possibilities they carry have been squeezed out by the distraction of all our devices. They've been erased by all the things that make people feel helpless, like life has happened to them.

This is tragic, but it is also completely unacceptable to sit there and do nothing about it. To play the victim. Only you can create the life you want for yourself—no one is going to do it for you. If you don't know what that life looks like yet, for whatever reason, that's fine. We're here now. The choices you make from here on out are what matters. And right now, there are two things you should do.

First, create little goals for yourself. Don't worry about the big, broad stuff for now. Focus on making improvements and banking achievements one day at a time. They can be exercise goals, nutrition goals. They can be about networking or reading or getting your house organized. Start doing things you like to do or that make you proud of yourself for having completed them. Do those things every day with a little goal attached to them, and then notice how doing that changes what you pay attention to. All of a sudden you will find yourself looking at things differently.

Once you've developed a rhythm with those little daily goals, create weekly and then monthly goals. Instead of zooming in from a broad place, build out your life from this small beginning and let your vision open up in front of you from there. As it does, and the sense of uselessness starts to loosen its grip, that's when you take the second step: put the machines away and create space and time in your life, however small or short in the beginning, for inspiration to find its way in and for the discovery process to happen.

I know this isn't as easy as it sounds. Life gets crowded and complicated as you get older. It can be hard to find space and time and not feel like you're trading off some bigger set of responsibilities, especially now that you've got these little daily, weekly, and monthly goals that you're crushing. And guess what, it is hard at first. But do you know what's harder? Living a life you hate. That's hard. This, by comparison, is a walk in the park.

Which it literally could be. Many of history's greatest thinkers, leaders, scientists, artists, and entrepreneurs found some of their greatest inspiration going for walks.

Beethoven used to take walks carrying blank pages of sheet music and a pencil. The Romantic poet William Wordsworth used to write as he took walks around a lake where he lived. Ancient Greek philosophers like Aristotle would lecture their students while taking long walks with them, often working out their ideas at the same time. Two thousand years later, the philosopher Friedrich Nietzsche would say, "It is only ideas gained from walking that have any worth." Einstein refined many of his theories about the universe while walking around the Princeton University campus. The writer Henry David Thoreau would say, "The moment my legs begin to move, my thoughts begin to flow."

Those are some pretty impressive people who saw the power of creating time and space in their everyday lives to take a walk. But you don't need to be a genius or a prodigy for walking to be useful or transformative. There is a lot of evidence for the power of taking a walk to increase creativity, inspire new ideas, and change people's lives, whoever they are. A 2014 study by researchers at Stanford University showed that walking increased the creative thinking of 100 percent of the study participants who were asked to walk while completing a series of creative tasks. There is a ton of anecdotal evidence as well. Do a quick Google search for the words "walk" and "change," and you will see an avalanche of articles with titles like "How Taking a Walk Changed My Life." They're written by all sorts of people: men and women, young and old, fit and out of shape, students and professionals, American, Indian, African, European, Asian, you name it.

Going for a walk helped them change their routines and their habits; it helped them shake loose solutions to tricky problems; it helped them to process trauma and make big life decisions. For an Australian man named Jono Lineen, it did all those things. When he was thirty, he decided to walk the entire length of the western Himalayas—nearly seventeen hundred miles—solo. The first to ever do it alone. It was a test for himself.

For months he walked, up to twenty-five miles a day, with nothing but his thoughts and the massively beautiful Himalayas all around him. He couldn't escape either of them. Eventually, he had a breakthrough. He wasn't there to test himself, he was there to fix himself. "I came to realise that what I was actually doing there in the mountains was coming to terms with the death of my younger brother," he wrote in an article in 2021 about his experience. He'd suffered in the years after his brother's death. He found himself stuck down a rabbit hole of sadness, and this simple yet difficult experience walking the Himalayas provided some clarity that pulled him out of it.

Years later Jono had another transformative experience, this time walking the five-hundred-mile Camino de Santiago de Compostela, the famous Catholic pilgrimage across northern Spain. "I was trapped in a very stressful job in London and I needed a break," he said. By the end of the Camino, after nearly three weeks of walking across fields, through small towns, up and over mountains and valleys, he'd made the decision to quit his job. "The change threw my life in a new and wonderful direction, and I'm thankful to walking for helping me achieve that."

Jono's experience isn't unique. More than three hundred thousand people from all over the world walk the Camino every year, less than a third of them for purely religious reasons. The vast majority have other reasons. Reasons like Jono's. Reasons like yours, probably. They're searching for inspiration, they're looking to make some kind of change, and what better way to find it than by taking a walk.

Over the years, I've used the gym as a place to think. When I go skiing, I use the ten or fifteen minutes in the chairlift as a kind of sacred space to let my mind wander. It's that way with bicycling too. No one can bother you on a bike, so you're free to let your thoughts go wherever they go. These days, I create space for inspiration by taking a Jacuzzi every night. There's something about the hot water and the steam, about the hum of the jets and the rush of the bubbles. The feeling of floating, of *not* being able to feel the weight of my own body, sharpens all my other senses and opens me up to everything around me. The Jacuzzi gives me twenty to thirty minutes of mental clarity. It's where I do some of my best thinking. Sitting in the Jacuzzi is where I got the idea for my speech to the American people after the events of January 6, 2021.

Like most people, I watched the riots unfold at the US Capitol on television and then in great depth on social media. And like most people, I went through a range of emotions. Disbelief. Frustration. Confusion. Anger. Then, finally, sadness. I was sad for our country, because this was a dark day. But I also felt bad for all the men and women, young and old, whom the cameras found, as television networks covered the historic moment and broadcast their angry, desperate, alienated faces across the planet. Whether they liked it or not, this was going to be the mark those people left on the world. This would be their legacy.

I thought about them a lot that night as I sat in the Jacuzzi letting the jets loosen up my neck and shoulder muscles, which were tense from the stress of the day. I slowly came to the conclusion that what we all watched that day wasn't the exercise of political speech, it wasn't an attempt to refresh the tree of liberty with the blood of patriots and tyrants, as Thomas Jefferson might say . . . it was a cry for help. And I wanted to help them.

Since 2003, that has been my life's focus. Helping people. Public service. Using the power that comes with fame and with political office to make a difference in the lives of as many people as possible. That was the direction my vision took for the third act in the movie of my life.

But this was something different. Something more. I was watching all these videos and reading real-time updates on Twitter and Instagram from people who were there. Protesters. Police. Bystanders. Reporters. If they could reach me through social media, I thought, then I could reach them.

Very quickly an image crystallized in my mind. I could see myself sitting behind my desk, with the sword from *Conan the Barbarian* in my hands, delivering a speech that cut through all the divisive nonsense between us, using my platform in a way I never had before. That Sunday, I gave a speech on my Instagram feed in the hope that, by talking directly to the people who were hurting the most, I could help them and maybe they could heal. I told my story. I talked about the promise of America. Then I held up the Conan sword, just as I had visualized a few days before. I described how that sword could be a metaphor for our democracy if we let it. I explained that the more harsh conditions you put a sword through during its creation—heating, pounding, cooling, grinding, over and over and over again—the stronger, sharper, and more resilient it becomes.

I called the speech "A Servant's Heart," not just because that's what we all needed to display to get us through such a dark moment in our history but also because I felt like I owed it to the country. Since I was ten or eleven years old, I'd viewed America as the number one country in the world, as the world's greatest democracy. Everything I had, everything I'd done, the person I had become—America made all those things possible. America is the only place on the planet where I could have turned my vision into reality. Now it was under threat, and with a servant's heart I wanted to protect it. A "servant's heart" also described the vision I was starting to develop for how to utilize my social media presence as a way to help as many people as possible, all over the world, and to do it much more directly than ever before. It was the evolution of a twenty-year vision of public service into a new fourth act that maybe would never have happened had I not made a habit of creating space every day to think and to let inspiration and new ideas flow in.

Going for a walk, going to the gym, reading, riding your bike, taking a Jacuzzi, I don't care what you do. If you are stuck, if you are struggling to figure out a clear vision for the life you want, then all I care about is that you make little goals for yourself to start building momentum and that you create time and space every day to think, to daydream, to look around, to be present in the world, to let inspiration and ideas in. If you can't find what you're looking for, at least give it a chance to find you.

## REALLY SEE IT

When I say that I could see myself sitting behind the desk in my office at home giving my January 6 speech, I really mean that. I could see it very vividly, like a movie playing in my mind. It has been that way my whole life, with every major vision I've had for myself.

When I was a boy I could *see* myself in America. I had no idea what I was doing there, but I was there. I could feel the tropical sun on my skin and the sand between my toes. I could smell the ocean and hear the waves—even though I'd never experienced either of those things in my life. The closest we ever got to waves was throwing big rocks into the deep water of the Thaler See, a man-made lake just outside of Graz, and watching the ripples flow outward. When I finally got to California, all my impressions turned out to be wrong, some for the better and some for the worse (sand sucks), but the fact that I had such vivid impressions at all was a big reason I got to California in the first place.

When I fell in love with bodybuilding, I didn't have vague hopes of becoming a champion. I had a very specific vision of it, borrowed from the pictures inside muscle magazines of guys like Reg Park celebrating their victories. I could see myself on the top step of the podium holding the winner's trophy. I could see the other competitors on the lower steps looking up at me enviously, but also in awe. I could see their tight smiles, I could even see the colors of their posing briefs. I could see the judges standing and applauding. I could see the crowd going wild and chanting my name. "Arnold! Arnold! Arnold!" This wasn't a fantasy. This was a memory that just hadn't happened yet. That's what it felt like to me.

As an actor, before I ever got my first starring role, I could see my name above the title on movie posters and theater marquees, just like I'd seen Clint Eastwood, John Wayne, Sean Connery, and Charles Bronson with their names above the titles of their movies, which I loved. From very early on, producers and casting directors were always trying to get me to shorten my name to Arnold Strong or some other such name, because they said Schwarzenegger is too much of a mouthful. It's too long, they said. What they didn't know, but that I could see plain as day, was that Schwarzenegger looks fucking great all by itself in BIG letters above the title of a movie.

It was no different with politics. For years, I'd had

wonderful experiences giving back to the community. I worked with Special Olympics athletes and at-risk youth in after-school programs. I was honored to be named chairman of the President's Council for Physical Fitness and Sports in 1990 and to travel around to all fifty states leading fitness summits aimed at getting our kids more fit. I was learning that I could have an impact at scale, and I started to kick around ideas for how I might be able to help even more people, including by going into politics.

The thought of running for office had been brewing for a while, but the vision for what that could look like was still unclear. The picture was out of focus. Do I run for Congress? Become a mega-donor? Some people had mentioned running for mayor of Los Angeles, but who in their right mind would want that thankless job? I couldn't see it. Then in 2003, the governor of California, Gray Davis, faced the prospect of a recall by California voters. The state was a complete disaster. People and businesses were leaving. There were rolling blackouts. Taxes were through the roof. Every week there was another story with bad news about California, and every week I got an-grier, hoping more and more that this recall election would happen. When it became clear that it would go forward, immediately the picture snapped into focus. I could see myself sitting behind the governor's desk in Sacramento, meeting with members of the Democratic-controlled Assembly, doing the people's work, getting California back on track. I was going to run, and I was going to win.

The picture in my mind was so clear you could have put a frame around it and hung it on a wall. It was incredibly similar to the vision I would have in January 2021 in that way. I could see the desk. I could see what was on the desk. I could see what I was wearing. I could see where the cameras would go and where the lighting should be. I could see and feel the Conan sword in my hands. I could hear how my voice would rise and fall as I addressed the big problems we faced and outlined my solutions for them.

Before I go any further, I recognize that this sounds like a lot of woo-woo manifestation mumbo jumbo, like The Secret and all those law of attraction books being peddled by bullshit artists. This isn't that. I'm not saying if you just visualize what you want, then it will come true. Hell no. You have to plan and work and learn and fail and then learn and work and fail some more. That's just life. Those are the rules.

What I am saying is that if you want your vision to

stick, if you want to increase the chances of success looking exactly like you hoped it would when you first figured out what you wanted your life to look like, then you need to get crystal clear on that vision and tattoo it to the inside of your eyelids.

You need to SEE IT.

Elite athletes understand this. They are masters of visualizing their goals. In fact, visualization has been the difference between the good and the greatest performers at the highest level of nearly every major international sport. The Olympic swimmer Michael Phelps was famous, all the way back as a teenager, for visualizing his split times down to the tenth of a second during training and nailing them lap after lap. Before every single shot, the Australian golfer Jason Day steps back behind his ball, closes his eyes, and visualizes his approach—from his address, to his backswing, all the way through contact, and picturing the ball hitting where he's aimed. During his multiple world championship seasons, the German Formula One driver Sebastian Vettel was known for sitting in his car before qualifying sessions with his eyes closed visualizing every turn, every gear shift, every acceleration and braking zone. Nowadays, nearly every driver on the Formula One grid can close their eyes, put their hands out in front of them like they're holding a steering wheel, and take you through a hot lap on the circuits they visit every season.

The reason they do this is because to do what they do at a high level is incredibly difficult. Just to get into the elite ranks and be competitive takes an insane amount of effort and skill and practice. If you want to win, you need more than just ability and desire. You can't hope your way into the winner's circle. You need to see your way there. If you watch most great mixed martial artists train, at the end of a three- or five-round sparring session they will get up and circle the mat with their arms raised in victory. They are visualizing the outcome of their next fight. "What you can 'see' you can 'be,'" as the sports psychologist Don Macpherson has famously said. You need to be able to see what you want to achieve before you do it, not as you do it. That's the difference.

As important as it is to know what success looks like, it's equally important to know what it doesn't look like. There are a lot of things you can end up settling for in this world that will get you a knockoff version of your goals, but that ultimately knock you off course, if the mental picture you have of your life is even a little bit blurry. Knowing what is and isn't success brings crystal clarity to your vision. And with that clarity, I have found, comes a sense of calm, because almost every question becomes easier to answer.

In 1974, after I won my fifth Mr. Olympia contest in a row, I got a call from the original fitness pioneer: Jack LaLanne. Jack invented a number of exercise machines as well as the concept of health clubs. He had about two hundred clubs at the time, and he wanted me to be their spokesman. I would be a fitness ambassador of sorts, doing promotional tours and some advertisements. They offered to pay me $200,000 a year. That was a lot of money in 1974. It's still a lot of money. Back then, the best bodybuilders in the world made $50,000 a year at most. It was a fantastic offer. And I turned it down without a second thought.

Being a national spokesman for a health club franchise was not part of my vision. I didn't think it was embarrassing or beneath me, or anything like that. Jack LaLanne was a hero to anyone who cared about physical fitness. The problem was that accepting his offer would prevent me from doing movies, which is where my vision was taking me by this point in my bodybuilding career. Knowing that made saying no very easy. I was comfortable with the idea of turning down all that money and the different type of fame the job would bring. I was calm, knowing that I'd just sidestepped something that was an amazing opportunity but also a big distraction.

If you can't fully see your vision—if you can't picture what success is and what it isn't—it becomes very hard to assess opportunities and challenges like this. It becomes next to impossible to know for certain if they'll get you what you want or something close, and if "close" is good enough for you. Having a clear picture in your mind is what will help you figure out if this thing you're about to do, if this choice in front of you, is the difference between ordering Coke and getting Pepsi, or between taking your dream vacation to Hawaii and landing in Guam. They're both islands in the Pacific, they both have nice weather, they both use the dollar, but only one of them has a Four Seasons.

Sports is much less forgiving. Settling for something that is almost your goal, that is in the ballpark, is the difference between winning and losing. Nobody gets into sports to *not* win. So why would you go through life to *not* aim for exactly what you want? This life isn't a dress rehearsal, it's not a practice or a training session, it's the real thing. It's the only one you have. So see it . . . and then be it.

# LOOK IN THE MIRROR

What do you see when you look in the mirror? A winner or a loser? Someone who's happy or someone who's miserable? Someone with vision or someone who's lost? Here's an easier one: what color are your eyes? And don't tell me they're blue or brown or whatever. Those are bullshit answers for your driver's license. What color are they, *really*?

Not so simple, right?

These are difficult questions for a lot of people. Most people hate looking in the mirror. And when they do, they almost never look themselves in the eyes. It's too uncomfortable. Too scary. Because the person in the mirror is often a stranger who looks nothing like the person they see when they close their eyes and picture the person they want to be.

As uncomfortable as it can be, you have to look at yourself in the mirror every day in order to know where you stand. You have to check in with yourself if you want to be sure that you're moving in the right direction. You have to make sure that the person looking back at you is the same one you see when you close your eyes and visualize the person you are trying to become. You need to know whether or not your vision aligns with the reality of your choices.

You have to do this to avoid becoming lost and useless, obviously. But you also have to do it to avoid becoming a bad person. In my experience, the fitness world, Hollywood, and politics are full of amazing people. I've met many of them. They're also full of douchebags, pricks, and assholes. I've met a lot of them too. Each one worse than the one before. You think gym owners can be sketchy and tightfisted, wait until you meet a studio executive with lots of money and no taste, or a politician who thinks the world revolves around them because forty thousand people voted for them in some small corner of your state. Navigating the gross parts of these worlds was like trying to move inside a set of Russian nesting dolls full of shit and hair gel. And the thing is, it's very easy to get swallowed up by them if you aren't sure of yourself and sure of what you're trying to accomplish.

The difference between the good ones and the bad ones is simple and obvious: it's self-awareness and clarity of vision. The good ones know specifically what they are trying to achieve, and they're disciplined about measuring their choices against that vision. They check in with themselves on a regular basis. Their vision changes as they change. It grows and evolves with them. The good ones aren't afraid of the mirror.

The bad ones—they avoid the mirror like the plague. Many of them let go of their vision a long time ago, and as a result the most superficial, self-centered version of the vision grabbed ahold of them and took them for a ride. They never did the work to clarify their goals or zoom in on what their world might actually look like in real life if they succeeded. They never felt the need to. These are the people who went into finance because all they wanted was to be rich. They went to Hollywood because they wanted to be famous. They got into politics because they wanted to be powerful. And their vision never went any deeper or further than that, because the earliest, broadest version of it worked for them. They'd achieved success in the one dimension that mattered to them in the beginning, and hey, if it ain't broke, don't fix it, right? Even when it's not working for everyone else around you.

I spent my entire adult life looking in the mirror. For the last twenty years, as a public servant and a philanthropist, the mirror took the form of votes, polling numbers, statistics, and data. As governor of California, as chairman of the President's Council for Physical Fitness and Sports, as a climate activist, there is no avoiding the numbers. The people will show you, with their words and their votes and their actions, what they think of you and your ideas. They will tell you whether or not they believe you or believe *in* you. You find out very fast whether your vision is real or a fantasy when the data comes in, when the needle moves.

The twenty years before that, in Hollywood, it was the camera and the movie screen that were the mirror. Whatever vision I had in my mind for the performance I wanted to give in a film, it pales in comparison to what five hundred people sitting together in the dark saw when I was thirty feet tall on the screen in front of them. The camera doesn't lie. It films in high definition, in full focus, at twenty-four frames per second. In *The Terminator*, I was only onscreen for twenty-one minutes, but that's still more than thirty thousand distinct images captured forever. What I thought I was doing in those scenes only mattered if the audience saw the same thing. Only then could I claim success. Only then could I say that I'd achieved my vision as an actor in that film.

The twenty years before that, as a bodybuilder, the mirror was a literal mirror. I looked in the mirror every day. For hours. It was part of the job. The mirror was an essential tool. You can't know if an exercise is working properly unless you watch yourself do it in the mirror. You can't know if a muscle has achieved enough mass or enough definition until you flex in the mirror. You can't know if you have all your moves down until you stand in front of the mirror and hit all your poses one after the other.

In the opening scene of *Pumping Iron*, Franco Columbu and I are in a ballet studio in New York City learning about movement from a ballet instructor. We're trying to get better at posing. She moves us through different body positions, adjusting our posture and our eyeline, smoothing out our transitions to make everything look more fluid and impressive. As she worked with us, she made an amazing point about paying attention to how we moved between poses. Onstage, the judges aren't just watching you at the key moments when you're fully flexed, when you're at your best. "What you have to realize," she said, "is that people are watching you all the time." She was so right! The static poses might be what end up in photos in magazines. They might be how people who weren't there will know about you. But the people in the room, the people who matter, will be watching and judging every aspect of how you move and how you transition between those key moments.

It was a perfect metaphor. Life isn't just the high points or the big moments. It's not just the stuff that ends up seared into people's memory banks or recorded in photos that are confined to scrapbooks. Life is also those stretches of time in between. Life happens as much in the transitions as it does in the poses. It's all one long performance, and the greater the impact you want that performance to have, the more important each one of those little moments becomes.

What you don't see in that first scene, because of the camera angle, is that the other two walls of the instructor's studio are nothing but mirrors. Like bodybuilders, dancers know. You can't grow unless you watch yourself do the work. You can't get better unless you judge your effort against what you know it should look like, in your heart and in your mind. To give the performance of a lifetime, to achieve any kind of vision, no matter how insane or impossible, you need to be able to see what the world sees when they're watching you try to achieve it. That doesn't mean conforming to the world's expectations, it means not being afraid to stand in front of the mirror, look yourself in the eyes, and really *see*.

# CHAPTER 2

# NEVER THINK SMALL

By the end of 1987, I'd killed 283 people. More than anyone else in Hollywood during that time, by far. It took me eight films, but I did it. And that meant something.

It meant that I was an action movie star. My name was above the title of most of my films. In big block letters just like I'd envisioned:

## SCHWARZENEGGER

I'd made it. That's what everybody said. Journalists. Studio executives. Agents. My friends. They talked to me like the work was over. Like there was nothing left for me to prove. "So, what's next for Arnold?" they would ask, sounding amazed at how far I'd come, and as if they couldn't possibly imagine there was anything more to do.

They were thinking too small. My goals had evolved. They were always growing. Another, bigger picture had snapped into focus for me. I didn't just want to be an action star who got top billing. I wanted to be a leading man. I wanted to be the highest-paid actor in the business.

To do that, I needed to show people that there was more to me than muscles and mayhem. I had to show them my soft side, my dramatic side, my funny side, my *human* side. I had to do comedies.

Nobody thought this was a good idea. Journalists thought I wouldn't be any good. Studio executives didn't think audiences would buy it. My agents thought I'd have to take a pay cut. Some of my friends thought I'd embarrass myself.

I begged to differ.

The year before, I'd become friends with the brilliant comedic producer and director Ivan Reitman. I told him about my vision and what I wanted to do. He'd seen all these other sides of me that I now wanted to show the rest of the world. And he could see it. He could see what I saw when I pictured the next step of my journey.

Ivan also understood that the Hollywood system is full

of naysayers. Their instinct would be to keep me in my lane, because that was the easiest thing for them to understand. *Arnold is an action star, so send him scripts for more action movies.* I couldn't go to a bunch of executives and ask them to consider me for their next big studio comedy. If I wanted to star in a comedy, I would have to bring the project to them and make it impossible for them to say no. So that's what we did. Ivan got a couple of writer friends of his to come up with some ideas, then Ivan and I got together and worked on them until we found one that we both liked and we both believed the studios would love.

That idea became *Twins.* A buddy comedy about twin brothers, Julius and Vincent, who were engineered in a lab and separated at birth, then found each other thirty-five years later. I would play Julius, the "perfect" one. Vincent, a petty criminal whom Julius bails out of jail when they first meet, would be played by Danny DeVito.

We were an amazing team. I'd just come off *Commando* and *Predator.* Danny had just done the *Romancing the Stone* movies after five seasons on *Taxi.* And Ivan had just directed *Ghostbusters.* Who wouldn't want to make a funny movie with us?

It turns out, most of Hollywood. Everyone loved the concept, but some studio executives couldn't get over the idea of me as a comedic lead. They didn't think I could pull off the role next to Danny, who was a comedy genius. Others thought I couldn't pull it off, period, regardless of who played opposite me. And then there were those who got the idea and loved the comedic potential of our partnership, but couldn't handle the price tag when they weighed it against the possibility of failure. All three of us were at the top of our game; we didn't come cheap. If the studio paid us our going rate, the movie would be expensive to make and it would have to do more than just succeed for them to make the kind of profit they wanted.

Ivan, Danny, and I put our heads together to come up with a plan. We loved the script, and we were confident that the movie would be a success if a studio gave us the money to make it. We just needed to find a way to turn one naysayer into a yea-sayer. Our solution was to reduce the studio's risk as much as possible by taking no up-front money. If a studio agreed to make our movie, all three of us would agree to make zero salary. Instead, we would take a piece of the net profits, called "backend" in Hollywood language. We would only make money if the studio made money.

We recognized that this was a big thing we were trying to pull off. In those days, studios almost never gave back-end to actors. (They still don't.) There was real professional risk for each of us with this project. And by deferring our compensation, there was financial risk too. But we thought, if we were going to do it, let's commit for real.

We found our yea-sayer in the form of Tom Pollock, the president of Universal. Just as Ivan saw in me what I saw for myself as a leading man, Tom saw what we saw as the potential of *Twins*. He even tried to get us to take up-front money, if you can believe that! But we held firm and stuck with the initial plan that got us to this place, and Tom gave us what we asked for.

By early 1988, we were in production down in Santa Fe, New Mexico. By early 1989, we'd not only had a presidential premiere at the Kennedy Center for President-Elect George H. W. Bush, we'd crossed $100 million at the domestic box office, my first movie to do that. To this day, people don't believe me when I tell them this, but *Twins* is still the movie I made the most money on in my entire career.

## *WENN SCHON, DENN SCHON*

There is only one person I have worked with in Hollywood who is crazier than me when it comes to thinking big: James Cameron. Jim and I have been friends for almost forty years. We've done three movies together. Two of them, *Terminator 2* and *True Lies*, were the biggest movies ever made when they came out. *True Lies* was the first film to officially have a production budget over $100 million.

But where Jim really stands head and shoulders above the rest of us is his ability to go all in on his projects. He's done it time and again. In German, we have a saying: *Wenn schon, denn schon.* Roughly translated, it means "If you're going to do something, DO IT. Go all out." Jim is the embodiment of that saying. He has always been that way, as long as I have known him.

I think it's something he developed as a model maker and a production designer early in his career. Those are two jobs where your goal is to make things look as realistic and as authentic as possible. To do that, you have to really commit to your task. You can't half-ass it. If you want whatever you're making to be believable, then "good enough" is never acceptable. It always has to be perfect. You can't miss a single detail. The big things and the little things matter equally.

It's the same way in bodybuilding, actually. There are four main judging criteria in every bodybuilding competition: mass, proportion, definition, and stage presence and posing. Within each of those categories, there are a thousand little things you have to work on in order to maximize your score. You have to be able to focus on both the big things and the little things if you want to win.

In Miami in 1968, I lost my first competition in America because I fell short in one of the four main categories: definition. The winner, a smaller guy named Frank Zane, was much more cut than I was. I was far too smooth. I'd missed a big thing. But then, after I moved to Venice a month later and started training at Gold's Gym, I realized that the reason I'd missed that big thing was because I was missing a couple of little things: my midsection and my calves.

The pros in America focused way more on the individual muscles of the midsection than we did in Europe. We did sit-ups and knee tucks, typical abdominal exercises like that to hit the upper and lower abs, but we weren't breaking down our workouts further than that— or at least I wasn't—to target the internal obliques or the transverse abdominus or the serratus muscle under the side of the pecs. You can see the difference in pictures of Frank and me next to each other onstage in Miami. I have a normal six-pack, which looks good, but Frank looked like each one of the muscles in his midsection was traced out of an anatomy textbook and chiseled from granite. I had to start doing what he and the other American pros were doing, only more and longer.

Then there were the calves. They aren't showstoppers like the big muscles (pecs and lats) or the "beach muscles" (biceps and delts), but they are just as important if you want to win. They're a big part of creating the symmetry of a perfect body according to the Grecian ideal. If you want to be great, you've got to deal with your calves.

Unfortunately, because they are slow-twitch muscles that are built to take a beating since we use them every time we walk, calves are notoriously difficult to develop. A lot of guys in those days really struggled to build mass there, so they either just accepted their fate or they forgot about them. It's easier to do than you think, since they're often covered by pants or gym socks, and it's really hard to get a good look at them, even in a gym mirror.

But I could see that mine weren't big enough. Calves are basically the biceps of the legs. I had 24-inch biceps. I did not have 24-inch calves. In my mind that threw my body out of proportion, which jeopardized my chances of winning Mr. Olympia and officially becoming the greatest bodybuilder in the world. I wasn't going to be the kind of person who let that happen. I wasn't going to let a small thing slide and risk it derailing my bigger vision. I came to America to be the best in the world. If I was going to do this, I was going to *do it*.

The day I realized this about my calves, I cut the legs off all my sweatpants so I couldn't avoid seeing them in the mirror while I worked out other muscle groups. Then I started working my calves every day. It used to be the last thing I did before I left the gym, now it was the first thing I did when I came in. A thousand pounds on the calf raise machine for dozens of reps. Seven days a week. Not only could I not avoid looking at my calves as I walked around the gym, now my competitors couldn't avoid seeing them either as they started to grow.

A year later I won my first of seven Mr. Olympia titles. Did all those sets of ab exercises and calf raises make the difference? Probably yes. But I guarantee you they would have made the difference if I *hadn't* done them.

Jim gets this. It's one of the reasons *Titanic* cost $200 million to make, more than any movie ever made to that point. When he started thinking about making *Titanic*, he wanted to tell the story of the world's most famous shipwreck in a way no one had ever experienced it before, because *he* had experienced it like almost no one else ever had. In 1995, he went all out and all in. He dove to the ocean bottom in a Russian submersible and saw the wreckage of the *Titanic* with his own eyes. He wanted the audience to feel what he felt when he saw it. He wanted them to feel like they were right there in the middle of the North Atlantic, going down with the ship. He wanted to immerse them in the history and extravagance of the greatest passenger ship ever built. "It has to be perfect," he said.

So he made it perfect. He built his own *Titanic*. Inside a gigantic $40 million water tank right on the beach in Baja, Mexico. The ship was 775 feet long. A nearly full-scale *exact* replica. It had a front section that could tilt into the water and a large rear section that could detach and drop ninety degrees. Inside the ship, he built sets that could also tilt. On the outside, he built an elaborate camera and lighting rig onto a platform that he suspended from a crane, which moved them back and forth, and up and down, along the hull of the ship.

It was so ambitious. Combined with all the special effects work that had to be seamlessly integrated into the practical effects that he and his team filmed on the set, there were so many ways it could go wrong. If every detail wasn't exactly right, the movie could come off as corny or boring or unrealistic.

To pull this off the way he envisioned, Jim knew he had to go all the way. No compromises or cut corners. No half measures, no half-assing. Every single detail of the sets had to be historically accurate. The carpet, the furniture, the silverware, the chandelier glass, the type of wood for the railings—it was all exactly as it would have been in 1912. He had all the dishes stamped with the White Star Line emblem. He even personally met with all the extras and gave them individual backstories. He went all in, and then some.

Filming took seven months. The film debuted in the United States on December 19, 1997. It made $28 million on its opening weekend and crossed $100 million by the end of the year. By the end of its original theatrical release, *Titanic* would earn $1.8 billion at the worldwide box office, making it the most successful movie of all time. It held that honor for the next twelve years, until it was dethroned by an even more ambitious movie, Jim's next project, *Avatar*.

Did Jim's willingness and ability to go all in like he does make the difference for *Titanic* and then for *Avatar*?

I don't know. But I guarantee you it would have been the difference if he didn't.

This isn't just how you should think about chasing your goals, it's how you should craft them, too, no matter how big or small they are compared to other people's.

If you are the first person in your family to go to college, don't just go to get drunk and dick around and walk out of there with a piece of paper. Dream of learning something that will change your life. Dream of really bettering yourself. Dream of the dean's list, not just of the diploma.

If you want to be a police officer, don't just aim for your badge or your pension, aim for the captain's bars. Aim to do good and to be an example for others.

If you want to be an electrician or a car mechanic, don't just aim for having your own shop and then sleepwalk through trade school or take your apprenticeship for granted. Really learn your trade and work to become great at it so you can be an asset to your community.

If your greatest wish in life is to be a parent, don't just pay for things or think that providing is your only job. Be a great role model who raises healthy, loving kids who go out into the world and do great things themselves.

What I'm saying is, if you're going to do it, *do it*. Not

just because going all in might be the thing that guarantees your success, but because not going all in will absolutely guarantee that you fall short. And it's not just you who will suffer as a result.

It's like that cheesy motivational saying: *Shoot for the moon. Even if you miss, you'll end up among the stars!* Setting aside that whoever came up with it never took an astronomy class, the point is that if you aim for a big goal and give it your all and you come up short, that's OK because you've still probably done something pretty impressive: graduated college, become a police officer or a mechanic or a parent, and so on.

But the flip side of that is also true, and perhaps more important. If you only aim for the smaller goal, the big goal is automatically out of reach, in part because you are no longer motivated to truly go all in and focus on all the little things that make the difference between greatness and good enough.

If I am content with being Mr. Austria or Mr. Europe, I probably don't worry so much about the level of definition in my serratus muscles or about the size of my calves, and as a result, Mr. Olympia is never in the cards for me. If Jim is content making a fun adventure movie about the *Titanic*, he probably doesn't worry about the stamp on a teacup that the audience will never see or the history of a background extra who will never speak. And we never get *Avatar.*

This is not to say that being Mr. Austria or making a fun shipwreck movie aren't also worthy visions to have, or that simply having a diploma or your own garage or a child isn't something you should be proud of. It's just not an excuse to give less of yourself. Regardless of the size of your dream, if you don't push yourself, if you don't give it your all, if you don't cut the legs off your sweatpants when the situation calls for it, then you're only letting yourself down. "No man is more unhappy," the Stoic philosopher Seneca said, "than he who never faces adversity. For he is not permitted to prove himself."

## IGNORE THE NAYSAYERS

There will always be people in your life who doubt you and doubt your dream. They will tell you it's impossible. That you can't do it or that it can't be done. The bigger your dream, the more often this will happen, and the more of these people you will meet.

Throughout history, some of our greatest performers and creative minds have had to deal with people just like this, people who didn't get it. The author of *Lord of the Flies* was rejected by publishers 21 times. J. K. Rowling's original *Harry Potter* book was rejected 12 times. The great comic-book artist Todd McFarlane was rejected 350 times by different comic-book publishers. Andy Warhol gave the Museum of Modern Art one of his drawings for free, and they gave it back! The producers of *The Godfather* fired Francis Ford Coppola multiple times because they didn't believe in his version of the story. U2 and Madonna were both rejected by multiple record labels before they got their deals.

It's the same story in the business world. The founders of Airbnb were rejected by all seven investors they pitched when they first tried to raise money. Steve Jobs got fired from his own company. Walt Disney's first animation company went bankrupt. Netflix tried to sell to Blockbuster for $50 million, and the Blockbuster folks laughed them out of the room. Jack Ma, the founder of Alibaba, got rejected from Harvard ten times, and at one point couldn't even get a job at Kentucky Fried Chicken. The inventor of virtually every major technological advance of the twentieth century was mocked at some point for

being foolish or impractical or just plain stupid by somebody who "knew better." Arthur Jones, the inventor of the
Nautilus fitness machine, got a rejection letter from one
naysayer that said, "You want to have consistent and uni-
form muscle development across all of your muscles? It
can't be done. It's just a fact of life."

The one thing all these brilliant people have in common is that in the face of doubt and skepticism, they kept
going.

Naysayers are a fact of life. That doesn't mean they get
to have a say in *your* life. It's not that they're bad people.
They're just not very useful to someone like you. They're
scared of the unfamiliar and the unknown. They're afraid
of taking risks and putting themselves out there. They've
never had the courage to do what you're trying to do.
They've never crafted a huge vision for the life they want
and then put a plan together to make it a reality. They've
never gone all in on anything. Do you know how I know
this? Because if they had, they would never tell you to give
up or that it can't be done. No, they would have encour-
aged you, the way I am encouraging you now!

When it comes to you and your dreams, the naysayers
have no idea what they're talking about. And if they
haven't done any of the things that you're trying to do, the

question you need to ask yourself is: Why should I ever listen to them?

The answer is, you shouldn't. You should ignore them. Or better yet, hear what they have to say and then use it as motivation.

As I got closer to my last Mr. Olympia competition in 1975, I did a lot of interviews with journalists from different muscle and fitness magazines, as well as bigger media outlets. They all had the same two questions: Why was I leaving bodybuilding, and what was I going to do next? I told them all the same thing. I told them the truth. I had accomplished everything I'd ever dreamed of and more in the sport of bodybuilding. I no longer got the same kind of joy from winning bodybuilding trophies that I used to, and for me it was all about the joy. I wanted a new challenge. I was going to start promoting bodybuilding competitions instead, I told them. And I was going into acting, to become a leading man.

I can count on one hand the number of journalists who listened to me describe my acting goals and said something like Ivan Reitman would say ten years later: "You know what, I can see it." Very few people said anything like that. The rest either smirked and rolled their eyes or they openly laughed at the idea. Even some of the people standing around watching, like the photographers and the camera people, laughed too. You can hear it on some of the videos of those interviews that still exist.

But I didn't get mad. I welcomed their doubts. I wanted to hear them laugh when I said that I wanted to be an actor. It fueled me. I needed it. For two reasons.

First, like with achieving any big vision, breaking into acting is hard no matter who you are. The way I wanted to do it, with my background, was going to be extremely difficult. I didn't want to become just another character actor who drove around Los Angeles every day going to auditions for roles that had a couple of lines here or there. I wanted to be another Reg Park, playing legendary roles like Hercules, or the next Charles Bronson, playing an action hero who takes out bad guys. Early on, I would have meetings with casting directors and producers. They would listen to me describe what I wanted to do, then they would tell me I could play a tough guy, or a bouncer, or a soldier. They would say, "War movies always need Nazi officers!" like I should be happy about that or content with it. I remember one of the very first times I mentioned my desire to act, maybe before I'd even won my first Mr. Olympia, one of the guys at Gold's who was a TV stuntman said, "I can get you a job on *Hogan's*

*Heroes* right now!" On top of all the hard work it would take to become a good actor—acting classes, improv classes, language and speech classes, dance classes—I was going to need all the motivation I could find to overcome the resistance of these naysayers who were in positions of power or influence and stood in my way.

Second, I needed their doubt and their laughter, because it worked for me. Growing up in Austria, all forms of motivation involved negative reinforcement. Everything, always negative, from the earliest days of childhood. One of the most popular books of German fairy tales when I was growing up, for example, was called *Der Struwwelpeter*. It contains ten fables about how misbehaving children can ruin everybody's lives with horrific consequences. At Christmastime, when St. Nicholas visits your house to bring presents to all the good boys and girls, he comes with a demon-like figure called Krampus with huge horns, whose role is to punish all the bad kids and to scare them straight. In small villages like Thal, the dads would go to one another's houses on the Feast of St. Nicholas wearing a Krampus mask and scare the shit out of one another's kids. My Krampus was our downstairs neighbor. My father was the Krampus for a number of families in the village.

Krampus and *Der Struwwelpeter* did their job. They kept kids in line. But for a select few who were wired differently, that kind of negative reinforcement produced something else: motivation. Not to "be good," but to get out. To get away, to move on to bigger and better things. I was one of those kids who was wired differently. And ever since then, I have turned any kind of negativity directed my way into motivation. The quickest way to get me to bench press five hundred pounds is to tell me it can't be done. The easiest way to ensure that I would become a movie star was to laugh when I told you my plan and then to tell me I couldn't do it.

You have a choice with the naysayers you face on the road to achieving your goals. You can ignore them or you can use them, you just can't ever believe them.

# NO PLAN Bs

When I became governor of California in 2003, I immediately inherited dozens and dozens of naysayers in the form of the California State Legislature. Democratic members didn't want to hear anything I had to say because I was a Republican who wanted the state to live within its means without spending the next generation's money. Republican members didn't trust me because of my positions on the environment, gun laws, and health-care reform. It was a tough situation to step into, but I had to ignore it. I had to put their resistance to my ideas to the side. My job was to find a way to work with them all, to pass legislation that helped the citizens of California.

That meant compromise. Wherever we could find common ground, as long as I didn't feel like we were letting the people down or making their lives harder, I would work with the legislature on the bills whose objectives we could agree on. With time, leaders in Sacramento got to see that I was a reasonable and thoughtful person. I wasn't a partisan hack, I was on the level. We could work together. But in the course of those first couple of years trying to get things done, there was always a moment at the end of meetings that slowly brought a new vision for my work as governor into focus.

It would go like this: my team and I would sit down with a legislator to discuss a piece of legislation I was proposing. I would describe how much it would cost, how it would help the people in their district, and how appreciative I would be if I could count on their support. They would say how we've needed to do something like this for a long time, and they agreed that it would be good for their constituents. And that's when it would happen. They'd lean back in their chair and say, "I love it . . . but I can't bring this back to my district."

Being new to this kind of politics, I wasn't sure what they were talking about. What do you mean you can't take it back to your district? Get on a fucking plane, go back to your district, sit in your office, and meet with your constituents and tell them what we're trying to do up here in Sacramento.

If I bring this back to my constituents, they'd say, I am going to lose my next election to someone from my own party, because they're going to say my support of this bill is proof that I'm either not liberal or not conservative enough. I'm in a "safe seat," they'd say, and by supporting this bill I'd be making the seat unsafe . . . *for me.*

They were talking about the impact of being from a gerrymandered district. I was blown away when I learned how extensive gerrymandering was, not just in California but with electoral maps all over the country, at every level. And that it has been going on this way for two hundred years! When it became clear to me that one of the big reasons no meaningful legislation got done was the way electoral districts were being drawn—every ten years by the same politicians who would benefit from redrawn boundaries—I knew right then that we had to fix these maps. It became a huge goal of mine as governor.

You would think I was trying to take away their free supply of American flag lapel pins, judging by the reaction of people from both parties when I introduced a redistricting reform measure to the ballot in 2005. No one was happy about it. A lot of politicians were pissed off. Everyone said it wasn't possible, it won't happen, I couldn't do it.

That was their first mistake. When they won in 2005, and the redistricting measure was defeated at the polls, they acted like that was the end of it. They thought I would just give up and move on to something else, to other priorities.

This was their second mistake. When something like redistricting reform snaps into focus in my mind, when it becomes a goal for me, I don't let it go. I don't move on. I don't quit. And I don't compromise. There is no plan B. Plan B is to succeed at plan A.

Which is exactly what happened.

Over the next three years I brought it up again and again and again. I talked with anyone who was willing to have an open and honest conversation about gerrymandering. I solicited opinions from all sides about the best way to accomplish real change. For the 2008 election, I incorporated all that work into a new redistricting reform measure that was even more aggressive than the one I put forward in 2005. That one lost by 19 percentage points. This one won with nearly twice as many votes as the previous one got. In three years, we'd basically doubled voter support for redistricting reform and put the power of drawing electoral maps into the hands of the people.

This is what can happen when you think big with your goals. When you go all in. When you ignore the naysayers. When you stick to your guns. Good things can happen for you and all the people you care about at a level that others never thought possible.

Let me tell you something: Nothing good has ever come from having a plan B. Nothing important or life-changing, anyway. Plan B is dangerous to every big dream. It is a plan for failure. If plan A is the road less traveled, if it's you carving your own path toward the vision you've created for your life, then plan B is the path of least resistance. And once you know that path is there, once you've accepted that it's an option, it becomes so, so easy to take it whenever things get difficult. Fuck plan B! The second you create a backup plan, not only are you giving a voice to all the naysayers, but you are shrinking your own dream by acknowledging the validity of their doubts. Worse, you become your own naysayer. There are enough of them out there already; you don't need to add to their ranks.

## BREAK RECORDS AND BLAZE TRAILS

There's a story about Sir Edmund Hillary, the first person to summit Mount Everest. When he came back down to base camp, he was met by reporters who asked him what the view was like at the top of the world. He said it was incredible, because while he was up there he saw another mountain in the Himalayan range that he hadn't climbed yet, and he was already thinking about the route he would take to summit that peak next.

When you reach the mountaintop, it gives you a brand new perspective on the rest of the world, on the rest of your life. You see new challenges that were out of sight before, and you see old challenges in new ways. With this huge victory now under your belt, they all become conquerable. After Everest, Hillary summited more un-climbed mountains like the one he told reporters about. After the success of *The Terminator* and *Predator*, I made the turn into comedy and did *Twins* and *Kindergarten Cop*, which were each the biggest movie I'd ever done when they came out. After sculpting his *David*, Michel-angelo didn't stop creating, he painted the ceiling of the Sistine Chapel, one of the great masterworks of the Ital-ian Renaissance. After cofounding PayPal and revolu-tionizing online banking, Elon Musk didn't take his money and go home. He founded SpaceX and revolutionized space travel, then he joined Tesla and helped revolutionize elec-tric cars.

Fulfilling a dream gives you the power to see further and deeper—further out into the world toward what is possible, and deeper into yourself to what you are capable of. It's why there are so few stories about people who have done something big then just packed their bags and moved to a private island never to be heard from again. People who think big and succeed almost always continue to push and to strive and to dream bigger. Think about the last time you did something difficult, that you were proud of. You didn't stop doing stuff after that, did you? Of course not. That success gave you more confidence to do other things. *New things*. That's how all the greats are. They may not succeed at the level of their greatest achievement. The music world is full of one-hit wonders. There are plenty of writers who had only one great book in them, or directors who had only one great film. But they never stop working or dreaming. They never say, "I made it, my work here is done." As long as they are alive, they will be working to achieve the vision they have created for the life they want to live.

Thinking big and succeeding does something to us. It certainly did something to me. It became addictive, because I learned that the only limits that truly exist are in our minds. I realized that our potential is limitless—mine and yours! What's just as powerful, I believe, is that other people realize their potential is limitless, too, when they watch someone like you or me bust through barriers and blaze new trails. When we think big and make our own dreams a reality, those dreams become real to them too.

There had been nine failed expeditions to Everest over thirty-two years before Sir Edmund Hillary and his sherpa, Tenzing Norgay, reached the top on May 29, 1953. Within three years, four Swiss climbers would do it too. Within thirty-two years, the same amount of time it took to achieve the first successful ascent, more than two hundred climbers would reach the summit of Everest. The day before Hillary reached the summit, a Canadian weight lifter named Doug Hepburn became the first person to bench-press 500 pounds. For decades, 500 was a mythical number for the bench press. By the end of the decade, Bruno Sammartino would smash Hepburn's record with a lift of 565 pounds. I've benched 525 pounds myself. The unassisted record, which has been broken and rebroken numerous times since, is now well over 750 pounds.

I've seen this process play out in my own life. Before I came to America, nobody ever left Austria. Maybe you went to Germany to work in the factories. If you were really adventurous, you moved to London to work in business. But America? No way. After I won all those Mr. Olympia contests and then I did the *Conan* movies, I started to see Austrians and Germans popping up all over the place in Los Angeles. They'd come over to get into the fitness industry, into Hollywood, into all kinds of things they read about me doing in the same magazines I'd read about Reg Park in years earlier. Without even intending to, I'd opened the door to America for them, and to their credit these men and women walked through it.

Watching someone with a crazy goal give it everything they've got and then succeed is so powerful. It's like magic, because it unlocks potential we didn't even know we had. It shows us what is possible if we put our mind to something and then back that up with effort.

If Reg Park, a kid from a small factory town in England, can become Mr. Universe and then a movie star, why couldn't I?

If millions of European immigrants can come to America with nothing but a suitcase and a dream and make a life for themselves, why couldn't I?

If Ronald Reagan, an actor, can become governor of California, why couldn't I?

*And if I can do what I did, why can't you?*

Granted, I am a lunatic. I don't do anything like a normal person. I don't have normal dreams. My risk tolerance for big goals and new challenges is sky high. Everything I do, I do big.

As a bodybuilder, I worked out twice a day for four to five hours. As an actor, I did major movies that were huge gambles. In my first and only job as a politician, I ran the sixth-largest economy in the world. As a philanthropist, my focus has been on pollution in the environment. My goal is to help *fix the earth*.

It's just how I think. Big.

I often wonder what my life would be like if I didn't do everything that way. If I'd done things differently. If I'd dreamed smaller.

What if I'd stayed in Austria and become a police officer like my father? What if I hadn't found bodybuilding, or if I'd kept it as a hobby instead of letting it become a calling? I've tried to imagine what life would have been like if I'd listened to those producers who told me to change my name; or if I'd let the opinions of reporters affect me when I told them I was going into acting. What would it look like, I wonder, if "good enough" had been good enough?

I don't know. And I don't want to know. A life of smaller dreams that I half-assed, doing some version of what everyone else does? That sounds like a slow death to me. I want no part of it, and neither should you.

Why aim for the middle? Why settle for "good enough" before you've even done the work to see what you are capable of? What do you have to lose? It's not like dreaming up a big vision takes more energy than dreaming up a small one. Try it. Grab a piece of paper and a pencil. Write down your vision. Now cross that out and write it again, only bigger. See, the same amount of energy.

It's no harder to think big than it is to think small. The only hard part is giving yourself permission to think that way. Well, I don't just give you permission, I demand it of you, because when you're thinking about your goals and crafting that vision for your life, you have to remember that it's not just about you. You could have a huge impact on the people around you. While you are breaking new ground in your own life, you could be blazing trails for people you didn't even know were watching.

How big you dream, whether you give it your all, or whether you give in at the first sign of trouble—these things matter. They matter for your own happiness and success, obviously. But they also matter because it could make a real difference in the world, far beyond what you can directly impact yourself.

## CHAPTER 3

# WORK YOUR ASS OFF

bet you and I have a lot in common. We're not the strongest, smartest, or richest people we know. We're not the fastest or the most connected. We're not the best looking or the most talented. We don't have the best genetics. But what we do have is something a lot of those other people will never have: the will to work.

If there is one unavoidable truth in this world, it's that there is no substitute for putting in the work. There is no shortcut or growth hack or magic pill that can get you around the hard work of doing your job well, of winning something you care about, or of making your dreams come true. People have tried to cut corners and skip steps in this process for as long as hard work has been hard. Eventually, those people either fall behind or get left in our dust, because working your ass off is the only thing that works 100 percent of the time for 100 percent of the things worth achieving.

Take something that most of us can relate to: becoming wealthy. It's pretty remarkable when you realize that some of the least happy people you'll ever meet are lottery winners and people with old family money. By some estimates, 70 percent of lottery winners go broke within five years. Among the generationally wealthy, rates of depression, suicide, and alcohol and drug abuse all tend to be higher than for the middle class or the people who worked hard to build their fortunes.

There are a lot of reasons this is the case, but a big one is the fact that new-money lotto winners and old-money rich people never got any of the benefits that come from *working* toward a big goal. They never got to experience how good it feels to make money; they only know what it's like to have it. They never got to learn the important lessons that struggle and failure produce. And they definitely didn't get to reap the rewards from successfully applying those lessons to their dream.

Imagine if Sir Edmund Hillary had been dropped at the summit of Mount Everest by helicopter, instead of trekking to it over two months in the spring of 1953. Do you think the view from the top would have been as beautiful? Do you think he would have given a shit about that other, smaller mountain he saw in the distance when he was up there? Of course not! If you don't get to experience what it feels like to push yourself, to do more than you thought you were capable of, and to know that the pain you put yourself through will lead to growth that you alone are responsible for creating, then you will never appreciate what you have the way that same thing is appreciated by someone who earned it, who worked for it.

Work *works*. That's the bottom line. No matter what you do. No matter who you are. My entire life has been shaped by that single idea.

In my quest to become the greatest bodybuilder ever, I trained five hours a day for fifteen years. When I got to America, I took my workouts up a level and invented the double split, where I trained two and a half hours in the morning and two and a half hours in the evening, just so I could get two full workouts in each day. I needed two sets of workout partners to pull this off—Franco in the morning, Ed Corney or Dave Draper in the evening—because no one wanted to train that hard. They weren't crazy like me. At my peak, on my heaviest days, I was moving forty thousand pounds of weight *per workout*. That's the equivalent of a loaded semitruck. Most people didn't want to work like that. It hurt too much. But I loved all the reps. I wanted all the pain. So much so that my first trainer in Austria thought I was a freak. He was probably right.

When I retired from bodybuilding and transitioned into acting, I took those five daily training hours and allocated them to the work of becoming a leading man. I took acting classes, English and speech classes, accent removal classes (I still want my money back for those). I took countless meetings and read hundreds of scripts— the ones that were sent to me for consideration and any others I could get my hands on so I could learn the difference between a bad script, a good script, and a great script.

Then there was the specific work of each movie, beyond simply reading the script and knowing my lines. On *Twins*, it was dance and improv lessons. On *The Terminator*, it was becoming a machine: blindfolding myself until I could do every gun stunt with my eyes closed, and shooting so many rounds at the range that I no longer blinked when my gun fired. On *Terminator 2*, it was practicing the shotgun cocking flip so many times my knuckles bled—for what amounted to two seconds of screen time. I didn't complain. It was all part of the work required to break the mold and be a new kind of leading man—an action hero.

I then took that philosophy into politics. During my campaign in 2003, I devoured briefing books on every issue that was important in the state of California. Each one was filled with detailed memos written by top experts about obscure topics I never imagined I would need to think about, let alone care about or potentially make decisions about. Things like microstamping on gun ammunition and nurse-to-patient staffing ratios in county hospitals. After my morning workouts down the hill in Venice, I opened the doors of my home to anyone who was willing to teach me about governing, about policy, about the things that mattered to Californians. I was committed to living up to and following through on the promise I'd made to voters during my campaign to be a different kind of politician. So I took those five training hours that I'd previously dedicated to bodybuilding, and then to the craft of acting, and I turned them into a kind of immersion program for the language of politics and government. Every day, I studied and practiced like a foreign exchange student trying to learn the local language, reviewing my notes over and over again, and then speaking from memory until the words came naturally.

The purpose of all this hard work—all the reps, all the pain, all the follow-through, all the long hours—was the same in every phase of my career. It's the same for anything special you could ever want to do with your life, whether it's owning a business, getting married, being a farmer, becoming a watchmaker, traveling the world, earning a raise and a promotion, going to the Olympics, managing an assembly line, starting a nonprofit organization, whatever it is. The purpose is to be prepared. It's to be ready to perform when the spotlight turns on, when opportunity knocks, when the cameras roll, when a crisis arrives. There is value and meaning in doing hard work for its own sake, don't get me wrong, but the real reason is so that when the moment arrives for your dream to come true and for your vision to become real . . . you don't flinch and you don't falter.

## REPS, REPS, REPS

From my earliest bodybuilding days, putting in the work has always meant repetitions. Not just doing reps, but tracking them. At the local weight-lifting club in Graz, I'd write my entire workout on the chalkboard, down to the number of sets and number of reps, and I wouldn't let myself leave until I'd marked them all off. When I prepared for movies years later, I kept track of the number of times I read the entire script by making tally marks on the front cover, and I didn't stop reading until I'd memorized every scene. (The only time I ever forgot a line was the day Danny DeVito pranked me on the set of *Twins* by swapping out my lunchtime cigar with one filled with pot.) As governor—and even now when I give commencement and keynote addresses—I'd do the same thing on the front page of my speech drafts. I knew once I got to ten reps I could do a decent job delivering the speech, but twenty reps meant I could knock it out of the park. The words would feel more natural, like I was speaking off the cuff and from the heart. The more I practiced the speech, the more of myself would be present in the room, and the more likely it would be that the people in the audience felt connected to me and the ideas I was sharing with them.

The key is, they have to be good reps. Not lazy, distracted, arched-back, noodle-arm, bullshit reps. You have to use proper form. You have to complete the entire exercise. You have to give maximum effort. Remember, *wenn schon, denn schon!* It doesn't matter if we're talking about a dead lift, a press conference, or a run-through of an entire speech. You need to be all there, all in, every time. Trust me, I'm speaking from experience here. It only takes one slipup, one wrong move, one wrong word, to derail your progress and set you back.

The whole point of doing lots of reps is to give you a base that makes you stronger and more resistant to silly, unfortunate mistakes, whatever that means for you. The goal is to increase the load you're able to handle so that when it's time to do the work that matters—the stuff that people see and remember—you don't have to think about whether you can do it. You just do it. That all falls apart if you don't take the time to do things the right way. If you half-ass your reps and fail to pay attention to the details, the base you're building will be unstable and unreliable.

It's why in firearms training they say "slow is smooth, smooth is fast." It's why first responder types, like paramedics and firefighters, train obsessively and practice the fundamentals of their jobs over and over again until it becomes second nature for them. It's so that when the shit hits the fan and the unexpected happens—which it always does—they don't have to think about the run-of-the-mill, life-saving parts of their work, and they can use that little bit of extra mental space to deal with the situations they've never seen before without wasting precious seconds.

And while the stakes are much lower in most other areas of life, that principle applies equally across most of them. Take something like jazz and the saxophonist John Coltrane. Coltrane is considered one of the greatest improvisational jazz musicians of all time. He developed his own unique style, called "sheets of sound," that when he really got going could sound like he was playing all the notes at once. Playing with other jazz greats like Thelonious Monk and Miles Davis throughout the late 1950s and early '60s, there's no telling what you would hear come out of Coltrane's saxophone from night to night. But what you could count on during the day was his fanatical work ethic.

Coltrane practiced constantly. Another saxophonist from his era said Coltrane practiced "25 hours a day." He would regularly play through the entire 256-page *Thesaurus of Scales and Melodic Patterns*, which is the musical equivalent of watching someone like Bruce Lee do "wax on, wax off" and "paint the fence" for eighteen hours. There are stories of Coltrane practicing a single note for ten hours straight to get the tone and the volume exactly perfect. At home, his wife constantly found him asleep with the mouthpiece still in his mouth. He said in an interview once that when he was really focused on an idea, he would practice off and on all day and completely lose track of how many total hours he'd been practicing.

What he practiced in private and what he played in public seemed like they weren't even the same art form, but they were intimately connected. It was all his practice of the fundamentals that made the improvisational music he played onstage seem like magic. Practice was rigid and structured, predictable and boring. His playing was free flowing and spontaneous and brilliant. It was like he didn't even have to think about the notes, which he didn't. *Because he couldn't.* If his improvisational style was going to mesh with the styles of the other players on the stage, there couldn't be any delay. There were no precious seconds available to think. Like a paramedic at the scene of an accident or a firefighter in a crumbling building, he had to know what to do, where to go, and what move to make, *in the moment.*

If you're a sports fan, that's very similar to what it's like watching the best footballers, basketball players, hockey players, and ski racers practice their craft and then perform on the biggest stages. There are hours and hours of monotonous shooting drills every week. There are miles of skating and skiing and running focused on footwork, change of direction, balance, and shifting body weight. There are hundreds, if not thousands, of reps of dribbling and passing drills baked into every practice.

Audiences all over the world loved John Coltrane's playing for its intensity. You would hear people say, "Trane's on fire!" What few of those people knew was that his fire onstage was fueled by countless reps of the most lifeless, boring stuff possible, which he practiced when no one was listening. The same is true for Stephen Curry on the basketball court, Lionel Messi on the pitch, Alex Ovechkin on the ice, or Hermann Maier on the mountain. They are able to blow our minds when the lights go on because they've done all the shitty, hard work when no one was watching.

This is where we need to get to. This is what we have to do. We have to embrace the boring stuff. We have to nail the fundamentals. We have to do them right and we have to do them often. This is the only way we can build that strong base and all that muscle memory, so that performing when it counts isn't a question. It's the easy part.

## PAIN IS TEMPORARY

I would not be where I am today without the success of *Conan the Barbarian*, which wouldn't have been the commercial success or cult hit it became without the director, John Milius, kicking my ass all over Spain, where we filmed the movie.

The basic work of making *Conan* was hard enough. Then there was the hour of weight training every day to stay in peak physical shape, since I had no shirt on the whole time. Then I rehearsed each of my long speeches with a dialect coach thirty to forty times before shooting days. I learned sword play and fight choreography. I trained in wrestling and boxing for the pit-fighting scenes. I learned to ride horses and camels and elephants. I learned how to jump from large rocks, how to climb and swing from long ropes, how to fall from a height. I basically went to another vocational school, this one for aspiring action heroes.

Then on top of that, Milius had me doing all kinds of terrible shit. I crawled through rocks, take after take, until my forearms bled. I ran from wild dogs that managed to catch me and pull me into a thorn bush. I bit a real, dead vulture that required I wash my mouth out with alcohol after each take. (PETA would have had a field day with that one.) On one of the first days of filming, I tore a gash on my back that required forty stitches.

Milius's response: "Pain is temporary, this film will be permanent."

And he was right, which is why none of that stuff bothered me. Pain was simply the price of the work that had to be done to make a great sword-and-sorcery film, as they called them. And if I was willing to pay that price, it would bring me that much closer to my vision. To do great things that last, sacrifices are necessary.

That's the beauty of pain. Not only is it temporary, which means you don't have to deal with it forever, it tells you whether you've begun to give enough of yourself in pursuit of your dreams. If the work of being great or achieving something special hasn't hurt or cost you anything, or at least made you uncomfortable, then I'm sorry to be the one to tell you, but you're not working hard enough. You're not sacrificing all that could be sacrificed in order to be all that you could become.

Pain isn't just an indicator of sacrifice, though, it's also a measure of growth potential. In the gym, if an exercise doesn't start to hurt, then I know I haven't done enough to unleash the growth potential of the muscle I'm targeting. Reps build strength, but pain builds size. That's why I wanted the pain. That's why in pictures and video footage from the gym back in the 1970s, I was smiling all the time. I wasn't a masochist. It wasn't fun to squat six hundred pounds until I couldn't breathe and I wanted to puke. I was smiling because I was feeling the pain of the work, which told me that growth was on the horizon. With each painful rep, I was taking another step closer to making my bodybuilding dreams a reality. That made me happy, because that was the point of all this hard work, to win titles and stand on the top step of the podium holding the championship trophy.

I'm not the first person to realize this about pain. Not by a long shot. Muhammad Ali famously said that he didn't start counting his sit-ups until they hurt. "They're the only ones that count," he said. "That's what makes you a champion." Bob Dylan said there's pain behind every beautiful creation.

You probably already know that this is true. I'm sure you've heard some of those popular sayings that get at this message. *Get out of your comfort zone. Embrace the suck. Lean into the pain. Do something every day that scares you.* These are just different ways of trying to tell you that if you want to grow, or you want to be great, it's not going to be easy. It's going to hurt a little bit. Or a lot.

In the selection process for Navy SEALs and Army Rangers, instructors don't really start to test candidates until they're completely fucking miserable. They exhaust you, they scream in your face, they restrict your calories and keep you outside or in the water until you're freezing and you can't stop shaking. And that's when they try to drown you or break your brain with little tests of fine motor skills and teamwork. But even then, they're not really testing for competence. They don't actually care whether you can complete the task. They're testing to see whether or not you'll quit when the pain gets to be too much. They're not interested in skill development or physical growth. Skill development comes later. And they know a driven candidate will take care of the physical part on their own time. They're looking for character growth. Which, in the pursuit of greatness and grand visions, is sometimes the most important thing.

Nothing builds character like resilience or perseverance through pain. Nothing destroys character like succumbing to pain and quitting. That being said, enduring pain for no reason is stupid. Now *that* is masochism. But we're not talking about that kind of pain here—the kind with no purpose attached to it. We're talking about productive pain. The kind that produces growth, that builds a base and builds character, that gets you closer to achieving your vision.

The great Japanese novelist Haruki Murakami once wrote, "I can bear any pain as long as it has meaning." I've learned over the years that this is true: pain only needs to have meaning to you for it to be bearable.

Just before Christmas 2006, I broke my leg skiing in Sun Valley, Idaho. I snapped my femur. The thickest bone in the human body. It's hard to break your femur. It *hurts*. And it requires immediate surgery to insert a plate and screws, which also hurts. Two weeks later, I was scheduled to be inaugurated to my second term as governor. Typically, this involves a swearing-in ceremony with the chief justice of the California Supreme Court, followed by a speech. In other words, a lot of standing.

My team and the event staff recognized the difficulty all that standing would cause, so they offered to cancel the official ceremony and do the swearing in at home while I recovered. I wouldn't have it. So I had two options: I could load up on painkillers and deliver my speech, hoping I didn't slur like a lunatic, or I could refuse the meds and deliver the speech clearheaded, knowing that standing still up at the podium was going to hurt like hell.

I can deal with twenty minutes of pain. I can deal with a full day of pain. My leg was broken whatever I decided. And I was going to be in some degree of pain no matter where I was—at home on the sofa or onstage in Sacramento. Why wouldn't I choose the version of pain that included fulfilling my vision of leading California toward a better future? Part of that vision was sharing moments like this. It was standing up in front of the people to show them that I would always stand up *for* the people. I would follow through on my promises, even when it hurt. It meant a lot to me to be able to do that. The pain, as John Milius said, was temporary. The power of that moment, and the sense of accomplishment I felt after the brutal election the year before, will stay with me forever.

## FOLLOW UP, FOLLOW THROUGH

Ten months later, near the end of October 2007, California caught on fire. I went to bed on a Friday night with reports of a handful of fires having broken out across the state. I woke up on Saturday to news that it had exploded to almost three dozen. The worst of them, in terms of the threat to lives and property, were concentrated in San Diego County and would ultimately force the evacuation of more than a half million people, including two hundred thousand residents of the city of San Diego. Thousands of them would end up at Del Mar racetrack and Qualcomm Stadium, where the NFL's San Diego Chargers used to play.

It was a nightmare scenario for the state—a firestorm in a heavily populated area. We'd been war-gaming and scenario planning and emergency drilling for disasters like this ever since we watched the horrific tragedy unfold in New Orleans after Hurricane Katrina two years earlier. Government services at every level failed those poor people, and more than fifteen hundred people died as a result. I vowed that if we ever found ourselves in a similar situation, we would have the right people and services in place as quickly as possible, we'd know what was going on from the beginning, and we'd be ultraresponsive to the victims and the people on the front lines. That was the whole purpose of all our planning and our emergency drills.

Now, this is where a lot of people can get it wrong when

it comes to the work of someone in a position of authority. They will assume that because, as governor, I'd made sure we had a plan, and that we'd practiced for disaster, and that everyone knew their role, my work was done. Like the boss of a company or the manager of a team, a governor has lots of responsibilities. They can't do everything, the thinking goes. At some point they have to delegate and trust that the plan they've put in place will work and that the people they've hired to execute that plan will deliver.

Except you can't just expect that other people are going to do what you think they're going to do or what they say they're going to do. Especially at the moment of truth, whether that's the cusp of success or the brink of disaster. (Making your dream come true often requires the same effort as preventing a nightmare scenario from occurring.) Shit happens. Signals get crossed. People are lazy. Some people are just plain stupid. If you have a job to do or a goal you're trying to achieve, or you've made a commitment to protect something or someone, and it's important to you that everything happens the way it's supposed to, it's up to you to follow through *all the way*.

By Saturday afternoon, I could see that the situation in San Diego was about to become a shitshow. I could visualize it in my mind. There were too many moving parts spread out over too large an area, and events were changing too rapidly to stay on top of them. Evacuees were already streaming into Qualcomm Stadium as night fell, and we still didn't have cots set up or enough water, and I knew there had to be other things we were missing. We were going to have to get down there ourselves, I felt, if we wanted to be sure everything got done.

On the way down, we got a sense from the folks on the ground at Qualcomm of what they still needed: more water, obviously, but also diapers, baby formula, toilet paper, and a weird one: doggie poop bags. You don't realize it until you really dig into a situation like a disaster response, but the main things to take care of after basic shelter are caring for infants and elderly, and then sanitation. We immediately called the head of the California Grocers Association and he marshaled his troops to gather up all the supplies we asked for and meet us there with them.

When we got to the stadium, there were still no cots. Where were they? Who had them? Why weren't they here yet? My team and I asked everyone who might have an answer, and we told them to call everyone they knew who might have an answer. We found out, after a daisy chain of phone calls, that the cots were kept in a storage facility that had been sold by the person we made the original lease with, and the new owner had changed the locks, not knowing that one of his units was full of cots that were an essential piece of California's disaster response plan. And nobody had a key!

You can't make this stuff up. If we hadn't been there to ask questions, to follow up and to make sure everyone around us followed through on their part in solving this problem, those cots might still be in that storage facility. Thank goodness it was only cots we were trying to track down. It could have been much scarier, like it was over at Del Mar racetrack.

Just before we were set to leave Sunday night, I got word that seven hundred residents of a local nursing home had been transferred to Del Mar. That they were safe was a huge relief, but something about the situation stuck in my craw. Anyone who has seen the medicine cabinet of an elderly person with even just an average number of medical issues understands that their care is complicated. In an emergency, it's not so simple as putting them in a bed inside an auditorium on the infield of a horse track. So I swung by Del Mar with my team and checked in on things.

The first sign of concern was that there were no doctors on-site at this point. There was a single nurse, a man named Paul Russo, who was a Navy medic and a total badass. He was managing the care for all these displaced men and women. The second sign came when I was walking around as everyone was going to bed and one lovely lady came up to me, scared and a little confused, and said, "I don't know what to do, tomorrow morning I'm supposed to go for my dialysis treatment."

This triggered an avalanche of follow-up questions. How many other people needed urgent daily care like dialysis? How many of them would be better off in a hospital environment under the supervision of a doctor? What's the nearest hospital with space? How many dialysis machines do they have? Do we have enough ambulances to get everyone there?

We spent the rest of the night finding out the answers to those questions. It turns out we had a few dozen people who needed care, but there were no hospital beds within 150 miles to place them. So we started calling the heads of each of the branches of the military, all of which had bases in California. One thing you learn as governor is that every base has two things: guns and medical facilities. We found an empty wing in the hospital at Camp

Pendleton, the Marine base just up the road. We had beds; now we needed ambulances to get all these people there, which we found up in Orange County, sixty miles north. We worked out of our plane, through the night, sleeping a couple of hours here and there while we sat on the tarmac, waiting for confirmation that everyone at Del Mar who needed to be moved got moved. It was tedious work in difficult conditions, which is to be expected in a crisis, and only when it was done did we take off and head home.

This is how you follow up. This is how you follow through. It's about leaving no stone unturned. It's about dotting your *i*'s and crossing your *t*'s. It's about closing the loop and circling back. I don't even want to think about what might have happened to some of those nursing home residents if we'd done even 1 percent less than we did. And yet so many people are content to depend entirely on plans and systems, or to do the bare minimum asked of them, and then think to themselves, *This is all set, I took care of it*. No. Don't be a lazy fuck. Do the work. The only time you are allowed to use the phrase "I took care of it" is when it is done. Completely.

I am a follow-through fanatic. In a lot of ways, I consider following through the crux of the hard work that is necessary for important things to get done, because important stuff is never simple or straightforward. It almost always depends on timing, on other people, on lots of moving parts—and you can't count on any of those things. Ironically, follow-through is usually the easiest part of the work, at least in terms of energy and resources; yet it's almost always the thing that we either take for granted or let slip through the cracks. We say, "I want to do this great, fantastic thing," then we get the ball rolling, and we just expect it to keep rolling, simply because we want it to. As if hope and good intentions are worth anything.

We even do this to ourselves. You see it in sports all the time. A golfer in a greenside bunker doesn't follow through with their sand wedge and the ball goes nowhere, or it rockets across the green. A tennis player does everything right during a point, they get themselves in position to smash a backhand down the line, but they forget to follow through on their swing and the ball goes flying out of the stadium. The same thing happens to footballers who don't follow through on one-touch volleys into the box or on something as basic as a penalty kick. I see it happen in the gym too. I can't tell you how often I see guys on the lat pulldown machine, for example, who don't get the full stretch at the top of the movement or the full flex at the bottom of it. They literally don't follow up or follow through.

It seems like a small thing in isolation, but a lack of follow-through at any moment can cause you to lose a match or lose potential gains, just like it can cause you to lose out in life. It's an indication that you're not committing fully, that you're not going all out, that you're just going through the motions. This is a much bigger problem than you think it is, because if you accept a poorly executed shot attempt or a half-assed lat workout from yourself as good enough, then you're more likely to accept half-assed versions of other, more important things from yourself. Things like your output at work. Or how you show up in your relationship. Or even how you take care of your baby. The person who is OK doing four sets of ten shitty half reps on the pulldown machine is more likely to sloppily change their baby's diaper or forget their partner's order at their favorite restaurant than the person who struggles through five sets of fifteen painful but perfect reps, even if it takes them longer and leaves them exhausted. Especially then, I would say, because those people know how good it feels to work hard and do things the right way.

Woody Allen said that 80 percent of success in life is showing up. Before him, Thomas Edison said that 90 percent of success is perspiration. They're not wrong, but they can't both be right. The math doesn't work. I actually think it was the American country singer and sausage maker Jimmy Dean who nailed it. He said, "Do what you say you're going to do, and try to do it a little better than you said you would."

Follow up and follow through, fully. Do just those two things, which I know you can do if your vision means enough to you, and it will set you apart from the pack. Unlike the vast majority of people who say they're motivated to do something important or to make a difference, it will show that you're serious about doing the work to make your vision real.

# THERE ARE TWENTY-FOUR HOURS. USE THEM.

I have some more good news for you. We have something else in common besides our willingness to work. We each have the same twenty-four hours in the day to do that work. Everything else about our lives might be totally different—age, money, where we live, what we're good at—

but we have the same drive and the same amount of time. That's fantastic! It means there's nothing we can't accomplish if we put in the time and effort.

The questions you need to ask yourself are: How much of that time am I wasting? How much of it do I spend thinking about how I'm going to get started . . . instead of starting? How much of it do I flush down the toilet of social media? How much of it do I spend watching television, playing video games, drinking, and partying?

My hope for you is that you don't waste much of your time at all. Sadly, a lot of people waste a lot of time. The worst offenders are the ones with big, ambitious dreams who desperately want to change their lives, but when I ask them what they're doing to achieve their dreams, they spend twenty minutes explaining how busy they are. Not surprisingly, the people who complain the most about not having enough time do the least amount of work.

Let me put it another way: busyness is bullshit. We're all "busy." We all have things to do every day. Obligations and responsibilities. We all have to eat, sleep, pay the bills. What does that have to do with putting in the work to reach your vision? If it matters to you, *make the time*.

By the mid-1970s, I'd achieved a number of huge goals for myself. I'd gotten to America, I'd won the Mr. Universe and Mr. Olympia contests. I was generally considered the greatest bodybuilder in the world. But the work wasn't over. Once you've reached the mountaintop, you have to figure out how to stay there. For me, that was partly shifting my sights to Hollywood, which offered the possibility of even greater success, but before that I had to spend a good amount of time carving out a decent life for myself in Los Angeles while continuing to do the work required to stay in competition shape.

First, I created bodybuilding booklets and made a deal with Joe Weider that he didn't have to pay me for the photo shoots I did for his supplements or his equipment if he gave me a double-page spread in the middle of his magazines to advertise my booklets. Then I started taking classes, mostly in business, at Santa Monica City College and UCLA. To make some extra money, I led weight-lifting seminars, and Franco and I went into the masonry business and did bricklaying work all around the city. With my bricklaying and booklet money, I bought an apartment building and became a landlord. And when I finally began to make the move toward Hollywood more concretely, that's when I started to take all those acting and improv classes I talked about earlier. My dance card was full . . . including with dance classes!

Of course, I did none of these things randomly. Beyond the fact that they either made me money or would one day save me money, in every instance I had my goals on my mind. I did the bodybuilding booklets because they allowed me to reach more people, and for the sport to reach more people. It was also a way to help those who couldn't afford to attend one of my seminars.

I chose to do bricklaying because it was like an extra workout. I got to work on my tan and practice my English on people, and I got to enjoy the sense of pride that comes with building things. You have to remember, my goal wasn't just to come to America, it was to become part of America. Being in movies was key to that, but there are still walls and walkways standing in Los Angeles that Franco and I built together between workouts fifty years ago that I feel are a part of my legacy, along with my star on the Hollywood Walk of Fame and billboards with my face on Sunset Boulevard.

I took business classes to learn the language of American business and to hopefully become fluent in it. I also wanted to prepare myself for the business side of show business, so I didn't get screwed by agents or studios.

I bought an apartment building so I had a place to live and I wouldn't need to worry about rent, which has always been one of the major factors that has driven aspiring actors to take crappy jobs that weren't part of the vision they had for their careers. I didn't want to be a working actor. I wanted to be an action hero and a leading man. Having a roof over my head meant I could be patient and say no to all those offers for bit parts as a Nazi soldier or a skinhead bouncer.

When I tell people what my days were like back then, even when I explain to them why they were so full, like I just explained it to you, they're astonished.

"When did you have time to eat?" they'll ask. Most of the time I ate like anyone else would eat, I'll tell them. Or if I was pressed for time, I'd eat in the car on the way to the gym or when I was studying. I'd have my protein drink every morning in class too. And on those occasions when I actually didn't have time to eat . . . I just didn't eat. Missing a meal never killed anyone.

"When did you ever have fun?" others will wonder. I never wasn't having fun, I'll say. Why would I bust my ass like that if it wasn't fun? I loved training. I loved learning how to lay bricks, which Franco taught me. I loved meeting new people and figuring out how Americans do business.

"When did you sleep?" is a popular question. I'd grab a nap after my morning workout, or in the truck while the mortar set on a wall we were building, I'll say. But usually I'd just sleep when I was tired.

"Weren't you always tired?" That is always the follow-up question. And my answer is the same every time: no. Now to be fair, I've always had a lot of energy, even going back to when I was a kid, so there's a part of this that is genetic. But the bigger part, the more important part, is the one that so many people miss. When you're chasing a vision and working toward a big goal, there is nothing more energizing than making progress.

When a concept from one of my business classes clicked for me in my studies, I immediately wanted to go deeper. When I could hear my English getting better, I wanted to talk to people and practice more. In the gym, when I felt the pump, I knew progress was happening, and it made me want to lift until my arms fell off. Sometimes I would. I'd lift until I felt the pump, then I'd keep going until I really felt the pain, like Ali talked about, and then I'd keep going some more until I couldn't move. There were some days that this was the only way you were going to get me out of the gym. And while I was definitely physically exhausted, mentally I was totally switched on. I was excited and energized, because I'd just spent two hours moving closer to achieving my vision.

How could you possibly expect me to sleep at a moment like that?

This is the kind of headspace people are referring to when they talk about slipping into "flow state." Time expands and collapses simultaneously. You get into something, you start making progress, then boom, the next thing you know, you look up and it's the morning.

Writers, musicians, computer programmers, chess masters, architects, artists, anyone with a hobby they are truly passionate about—they all have stories like this. Stories of doing work that seem to defy the limits of human attention span and physiology, when at some point time should have caught up with them and shut their brains off. And sometimes that does happen, like Coltrane falling asleep with the saxophone still in his mouth, or a video-game designer passing out on their keyboard, or a detective falling asleep surrounded by case files. But just as often, you get software programmers going on thirty-six-hour hackathons, creating games or apps that change the world. Or you get a story like the director Sam Peckinpah rewriting the script of *The Wild Bunch* over three days in the desert. Or you get Black Sabbath recording their debut album in one twelve-hour stretch. Or Keith Richards coming up with the riff for "Satisfaction" as he's about to fall asleep after a long day in the studio.

Whether it's a matter of getting into flow state or not, what every person who gets shit done has in common is that they either find the time, make the time, or turn the time they do have into what it needs to be for them to accomplish the task in front of them. When you hear stories like these, if you're still worried about eating or energy or sleep or fun, maybe your problem isn't time at all. Maybe it's what you're spending your time on. Do you know how many times people tell me they don't have time to work out, and then I ask them to take out their phones and show me their screen time stats and it says they spent three and a half hours on social media? It's not hours in the day you lack, it's a vision for your life that makes time irrelevant.

Or maybe you do have an amazing, powerful vision that motivates you, but the time required to achieve it is so great that the journey toward success has become overwhelming and paralyzing. That's a real possibility, and it can be very scary. I get it. Building a body that would eventually win bodybuilding contests didn't happen overnight, or over a year, or even over two or three years. It took several years of constant, daily work that nobody was paying me to do in order to get my body to the size and proportion that would eventually get the attention of judges, Joe Weider, and the public. Then it took even more years to fine-tune my body and keep it where it needed to be in order to win consecutive Mr. Olympia titles and play roles like Conan and the Terminator.

If I'd focused completely on the end result or tried to swallow the elephant in one bite, as the saying goes, I absolutely would have choked. I would have failed. The only way to achieve the kind of sustainable, life-changing success that I wanted was to do the hard, incremental work day in and day out. I had to focus on doing the reps and executing well. I had to listen to the pain and build on the growth that would eventually come. I had to follow through, every day, on the plan I'd created in pursuit of my larger vision.

The same principles apply to you, whatever you're trying to accomplish, however busy your life currently is. Here, I'll prove it to you. Let's do an exercise I call The 24-Hour Countdown:

How many hours per day do you sleep? Let's say it's eight hours, because that's what all the current science says is ideal for peak performance and longevity. OK, now there are sixteen hours left in the day.

How many hours do you work in a day? Let's say that's eight hours as well. Now we're down to eight hours left in the day.

How long is your daily commute? The average daily commute in the United States is just under a half hour each way, but let's round up to account for people who live near big cities and say it's forty-five minutes each way. That's an hour and a half. Now we're down to six and a half hours left.

How much time do you spend with your family, including breakfast and dinnertime and watching TV? Let's put that at three and a half hours, which is great. That's real quality time. Now we're down to three hours left in the day.

How much time do you spend working out or being physically active each day? For most people, that usually averages out to about an hour, including walking the dog, doing chores, and working out. Fantastic, an hour a day of activity is so important. We're down to two hours.

After all this stuff in a typical daily life is accounted for, there are still two hours left in the day to make progress toward your vision. I can already hear the question coming from a bunch of you: What about time for rest and relaxation? First of all, rest is for babies and relaxation is for retired people. Which one are you? If you want to do something special, if you have a big dream that you want to achieve, I believe you're going to have to put relaxation aside for a while. But fine, you want some relaxation, take half of the remaining time for your little nap. That still gives you an hour each day to work toward your goal.

Do you have any idea how powerful an hour a day is? If you want to write a novel, sit down and write for an hour every day, and aim for just one page. At the end of the year, you will have a 365-page manuscript. That's a book! If you want to get in shape, burn five hundred more calories each day than you consume. In one week, that's a pound you will have lost. In a year, that could be fifty pounds! How can you burn more than you eat? Try using that leftover hour to ride your bike. Even at a moderate pace, even just five days a week, by the end of a year you will have ridden farther than the distance between Los Angeles and Boston. You will have ridden across the country!

These are fantastic accomplishments that require a lot of hard work. But it's work that you are more than capable of doing when you've planned it out and broken it down into little, daily goals that shouldn't take more than an hour or two to complete. Hell, you can even be crazy like me, and it's still only five hours of work each day. That leaves nineteen hours to do everything else. Eat a little quicker, hit the brakes on your commute a little less, and sleep a little faster and you'll have found the hours you need. So don't tell me you don't have time to train, or to study, or to write, or to network, or to do whatever you need to do to achieve your vision.

Turn your TV off. Throw your machines out the window. Save your excuses for someone who cares. Get to work.

# CHAPTER 4

# SELL, SELL, SELL

**O**ne of the bigger culture shocks I experienced coming to America was the lack of awareness in the culture about bodybuilding. From everything I'd read about the sport in Joe Weider's magazines, I was expecting much more than what I found.

Don't misunderstand me, the subculture of bodybuilding was definitely there. We had our magazines and nutritional supplements. We had our competition circuit with its different titles and trophies. There were great bodybuilding gyms all over the country, including two big ones in Los Angeles, where I was. And there were fans and groupies as well. But very few people outside of the bodybuilding community knew anything about the sport.

When I met someone at a party or interacted with a stranger in line at the store, and they saw how built I was (which wasn't hard since I walked around in shorts and tank tops all the time), they would say something like, "Wow, look at those muscles, what are you, a football player?" I'd say, "No, guess again," and then they'd say something like a wrestler or a bouncer. They would almost never guess that I was a bodybuilder.

I noticed that big newspapers and sports magazines weren't writing stories about bodybuilding. TV networks weren't covering us either. And when they did, they tended to cover a competition the way they cover events like Nathan's Famous International Hot Dog Eating Contest today. We were a curiosity. A novelty. You could feel it in how they chose to describe us. "Muscle-bound" and "freak" (or "freakish") were words that appeared in almost every story. They were constantly insinuating that we must be stupid or gay or narcissistic. This confused me. Why was being in peak physical shape so odd to them? And why were those the only choices?

Why were they fixated on our posing briefs or the oil we'd use to highlight muscle definition? They'd ignore the years of work and sacrifice we'd all put in, then they'd reduce a world championship competition to the simplest visual: a group of tanned, shiny men flexing next to one another onstage, very clearly overcompensating for what must be lacking inside the very little clothing we had on.

I asked some of the American guys at Gold's why it was like this. They didn't know. "We should talk to these journalists!" I said, but most of the guys wanted no part of that. They said all those writers and reporters were prejudiced or jealous, that's why they were always so unfair to us. "Why would this time be any different?" they said. But that didn't make sense to me. How would a writer know how many hours a day we work? How would they know how much we lift or how strong we are or how disciplined we have to be? How would they know any of this stuff if we didn't tell them? My bodybuilding peers didn't want to talk to journalists because they continually mischaracterized who we were and what we did, but *not* talking to them was how we got ourselves into this position of misunderstanding in the first place.

I was one of the youngest guys in the gym in those days, but I'd had enough experience doing sales-type jobs back in Europe to know that if you're trying to get exposure for something and grow your business—even if that business is an unconventional sport—you have to tell people about it. You have to communicate and promote so that people know it exists. So they know what it's all about and why they should care. In other words, you need to sell it.

That's our job, I told the guys, to articulate what body-building is to the public.

Newspapers, TV shows, journalists? They shouldn't be our enemy, they should be our partners. They need stories to fill up their pages and their air time just as much as we need to get our story out there. If we want the sport to be big, we should be filling those buckets of space for them with our own descriptions of our sport and our own ideas about what makes it special. We couldn't expect them to fill those buckets the way we could, and we certainly couldn't count on them to fill that space the way we wanted them to. Just look at what happened when they were left to their own devices. If we wanted to change the image of bodybuilding, we had to be the ones to educate the journalists, and therefore the public. We had to be the ones to explain the sport to them, to promote it, to *sell it*.

When entrepreneurs and athletes and artists ask me for advice nowadays—it doesn't matter if they're talking about their newest product, their latest piece, or how to get representation—the one thing I tell them that they should be doing more of is promoting. Communicating. Selling. *Sell, sell, sell!* You can have the most amazing idea, the most fantastic plan, the best in class of virtually anything, but if nobody knows that it exists or knows what it is, then it's a waste of time and effort. It might as well not exist at all.

When it comes to realizing your dreams, you cannot allow that to happen. In fact, it should never happen, because no one is better equipped or motivated than you to sell your vision to the world. It doesn't matter if you want to move your family to a different country or your football team to a new town, if you want to make movies or make a difference, if you want to build a business, buy a farm, join the military, or create an empire. No matter the size of your dream, you have to know how to sell it and who to sell it to.

## KNOW YOUR CUSTOMER

Selling your vision means being open about what you're trying to achieve and telling your story in such a way that it is perceived in the most positive light possible by the people you need or want to get a yes from. Your customers, in other words.

When I made the initial transition into acting, and then moved from action films into comedies, it was agents, directors, producers, and studio executives who I had to sell on my vision, so they would say yes and give me a shot in their movies. The whole dog-and-pony show that Ivan, Danny, and I did in Tom Pollock's office to get *Twins* made was just a sales routine for one big customer who was looking to reduce his risk. Our job was to tell Tom a story that made our vision for the film seem like exactly what he was looking for.

"Listen," I said, "we're all on the same page, believe me. We have the same creative vision for this movie. There are no egos here."

"I know exactly how to shoot this, Tom," Ivan said. "Just give us the sixteen million, and I'll bring this thing in on time and on budget."

"Then we can all share in its success," Danny said. "And you won't have to worry about salaries at all."

Tom reached across the desk and shook our hands. He understood that this was a great deal for everyone, and he was about to show us just how great a deal he thought it was for us. He pushed back from his chair, came out from behind his desk, bent over, and turned his pants pockets inside out.

"Do you know what you just did to me?" he asked. "You just robbed me blind and fucked me. That's what you did. Congratulations."

We all laughed. Another satisfied customer!

As I started to get leading roles, it was the media and the public who I had to sell myself and my movies to more than producers and executives. I had to show the movie-goers that I was good as an actor, and I had to convince the critics that my movies were good as pieces of art. And I don't just mean good in terms of quality, I also mean good in terms of good for society.

The first time this happened at a major level was when *The Terminator* was coming out. All that many journal-ists wanted to talk about was the violence in the film. After all the imaginary killing I did in the *Conan* movies, they questioned why I wanted to play a killing machine in my next role. It sounds almost quaint now, but you have to remember that in the early 1980s movie critics actu-ally mattered a lot. Critics like Gene Siskel, Roger Ebert, Pauline Kael, Rex Reed, Leonard Maltin—these folks could sink your movie with a bad review.

I made a conscious decision that whenever I faced those kinds of violence-related questions in interviews during promotion for the premiere of *The Terminator*, I was going to answer the criticisms directly. I asked one reporter whether they'd read the Bible and understood that, by body count, it's one of the bloodiest books ever written. I reminded another reporter that the movie was science fiction, that my character was a machine and represented a warning to the human race about technology. I explained that the script that Jim Cameron had written was, by definition, 100 percent pro-human. With every opportunity I got, I told the version of *The Terminator* story that was actually Jim's intention, not the one that all these random journalists seemed desperate to write. The end result speaks for itself: the movie was a box-office success and it got great reviews across the board.

I was fortunate that it was pretty obvious who I needed to sell to. If you take the time to understand your own environment, it can be just as obvious for you too. The people you need to sell will make themselves known to you, and you can put your focus on them.

Let's say you want to pursue your passion for throwing pottery. You have a vision for making beautiful dishes and selling them at the local farmers market or online through your own website. You don't need anyone to say yes to this dream. There are no gatekeepers to the world of pottery...unless you want to take out a loan to finance all the equipment and supplies you'll need. Then you need a bank (or a relative or a friend with money) to say yes, which means they are your customer now and it's your job to sell them on this vision.

But let's say you don't need to take out a loan; there's still the matter of the people who you want to get a yes from just so that you know they're on your side. In this case, that could be your partner or your parents, who are worried that if you quit school or quit your job you'll run out of money and you'll go broke. They aren't naysayers in the traditional sense, they're just scared—for you and for themselves. Your job is to sell them on your vision in order to reassure them and to move them from a potential no to ideally a yes, but at least an OK. Obviously you don't need their approval to pursue your dream, and you shouldn't let it stop you if their approval doesn't come, but if you can sell them it's always better to have more people in your corner.

As a teenager in Austria I learned a lot about selling in vocational school and as an apprentice at a hardware store in Graz. I did all the jobs you'd expect to do at a hardware store: deliveries, inventory and restocking, sweeping up, bookkeeping, customer service, and, of course, sales. It was on the floor watching the owner, Herr Matscher, where I learned the most about selling and why people buy the things they do—not just products and services, but ideas too.

Herr Matscher could sell all kinds of things to all manner of people, because he paid attention and tuned into them. I remember one afternoon a husband and wife came in to look at tile. Herr Matscher greeted the wife politely then turned his attention to the husband, which was customary in a culture like Austria's in the early 1960s, because he was the head of household. Herr Matscher pulled out a selection of tiles and laid them in front of the couple. He started explaining the positives and negatives of each color and style, directing his words to the husband. He asked the man whether he preferred one style over the other, one color over another. He asked what room the tile would be installed in, what his budget was, when they would need the tile. Very quickly, the husband got annoyed by all the questions, which confused me. All of Herr Matscher's questions were standard and necessary. A typical customer would be mad if they weren't asked these questions. Then I noticed Herr Matscher shift his body toward the wife. She was interested in his questions. She had opinions about the tiles. She was engaging with him and considering everything he was telling them.

Herr Matscher understood that he had been talking to the wrong person. The husband might be the one who was making the money, but it was the wife's opinion and decision that mattered. She had a clear vision for what they were going to do with the tile. Her husband didn't care, he was just there to make her happy and to write the check. He was the buyer, technically speaking, but she was the real customer. She was the one Herr Matscher needed to get a yes from. Immediately, he directed all his energy to the wife, and after an extended conversation that didn't include the husband at all, they arrived at a decision.

"What do you think, dear?" she said to her husband.

"Yes, yes, whatever you want," he said, without even looking at the tile she'd selected.

Herr Matscher presented him with the invoice for the total cost, and he wrote a check on the spot without asking a question.

"What did you just learn?" Herr Matscher said to me after the couple left.

"How to sell our merchandise," I said, unsure of what he was really asking.

"Yes, but that's just one thing," he said. "Did you see how I switched and started paying attention to the woman? I did that because she was in charge of that particular purchase. It came from her that they wanted tiles for their bathroom. It came from her what color they should be. So I put my focus on her."

"I noticed that," I said.

"When a couple or a group comes in," he said, "you need to figure out who is in charge, who is passionate about whatever it is you're selling, who is the one who engages the most with you. You need to know who is the customer, who is the boss, and who is making the decisions."

I will never forget that interaction and what it taught me about paying attention and tuning into people. You can never take for granted that you know who your customer is. It's not always obvious who you need to move toward a yes and who you need to move away from a no. Unless you pay attention to who is paying attention to you, it's impossible to know for sure who your vision is attracting positively or who it might be impacting negatively.

A big part of selling your vision is seeing how the world around you reacts to what you're trying to do. It's how you figure out who wants to say yes and who you need to say yes. If you can do that, you will know who all your customers are before they even know that you're selling to them.

# MAKE MOUNTAINS OUT OF MOLEHILLS

You are your first customer, when you really think about it. The purpose of getting crystal clear on your vision and thinking about how it's going to happen is to sell yourself on the possibility of your own dream. But eventually you need to sell the world on it too. One of the easiest, most authentic ways to start selling it is to speak your inner voice out loud so others can hear it. All those things you tell yourself about what you're going to achieve, you should start saying to other people.

For some, publicly committing to their vision is essential, because they get caught up in planning instead of executing. Dreaming is always easier than doing. Publicly committing to a big goal is a great way to get moving. It is also a critical step for the many of us who need people to know about our dreams in order for those dreams to reach their full potential. That could be opening a restaurant or an auto shop, or starting a political campaign—anything that needs customers or supporters of some kind. If you need people to know about whatever your thing is, you've got to tell them. And if you really want to supercharge your dream's exposure to the world, don't just tell them about it, act like it's already come true. You do that by talking openly about what you're working toward but removing the phrase "will be" from your vocabulary.

It's not "I will be a great bodybuilder." It's "I can see myself as a great bodybuilder."

It's not "I will be a leading man." It's "I can picture myself as a leading man."

They do this all the time in political campaign rallies. It's not "Please welcome to the stage, the man who will be the next governor of California . . ." It's always "Please welcome to the stage, the next governor of California . . ."

Saying things this way is very powerful for two reasons: First, it presents your vision to the world as if it were real, which puts you in the position of having to work hard *right now* to make it true. Second, in cases where you need other people to believe in your vision for it to reach the highest heights, making it sound like it's already gotten there is the ultimate marketing. To the people who want to be part of your company, or your movement, or whatever it is, giving them the sense that the dream has come true is like a call to arms.

This was the genius of Joe Weider and his brother, Ben. They didn't say, "Bodybuilding will be a huge sport one day." They said, "Bodybuilding is a huge sport," and they spread that message wherever they could. On promotional trips to other countries, trying to set up a network of international bodybuilding federations, they would tell local politicians, "Bodybuilding is nation-building." What a line!

As a young kid in the early 1960s, reading their magazines and looking at their advertisements, I had no reason not to think that bodybuilding was everything the Weiders said it was. It *must* be a mainstream sport with fans all over the world. Bodybuilding champions were in movies, after all. They were on magazine covers and in pictures with beautiful women in famous locations like Muscle Beach. They were endorsing products. That doesn't happen unless bodybuilding is huge, right?

Wrong.

When I got to Venice Beach in late 1968, I quickly learned that Joe had exaggerated things a little bit. Muscle Beach had been closed down for nearly a decade. Bodybuilders weren't walking around everywhere with surfboards under one arm and a blond girl in a bikini under the other. They weren't rich and famous either. Weider Nutrition, which I thought was a massive operation, not just at the heart of the bodybuilding industry but at the heart of industry, *period*, was really just a normally successful American company. They had a good number of employees in multiple offices selling an impressive quantity of product, but the planes with the Weider name on them that I had seen in his magazines didn't exist. He had rented a plane for a photo shoot and put a fake logo on it.

Still, that didn't matter to me. Joe had convinced me and millions of others like me over the years that America was where we needed to be to bring our visions to life and to take the next step on our journeys toward success. Los Angeles was also where I needed to be to take the step after that. Plus, as a hardworking twenty-one-year-old full of energy, the fact that I had to do a little more work than I imagined in order to make bodybuilding mainstream was no sweat off my back. Joe had filled the bucket well enough to grow the sport to the point that it drew me in and got me to America. Now it was my turn to fill the bucket, to sell the vision, and to grow the sport even more, and draw in everybody else.

I decided to hire a publicist, who helped get me on *The Dating Game, The Mike Douglas Show,* and, later, *The Tonight Show* with Johnny Carson. I did bodybuilding seminars all over the country to complement my training booklets in order to expand awareness and educate those who were interested. I made myself available to any opportunity to tell the story of bodybuilding the way Joe and I both believed it should be told, which included talking to Charles Gaines and George Butler in 1973 for their book, *Pumping Iron,* which set the table for everything that would unfold over the rest of the decade.

In the summer of 1974, I did an interview with a writer for the *Los Angeles Times* in which I got to debunk all the misconceptions about bodybuilding and explain what the sport was really all about. I sold the sport to the reporter much the way Joe had sold the sport to me through his articles. The result was a long, fair profile that called me "the Babe Ruth of bodybuilding" and included a full-length photo that ran on the front page of the sports section with a headline that boasted about how much money

I was able to make just from bodybuilding. A few months later, *Sports Illustrated* wrote a story about the Mr. Olympia contest, which was held at Madison Square Garden that year, and it was filled with the same kind of language that a sportswriter would use to describe the best athletes in the most popular mainstream sports of the day.

Not even two years later, the Mr. Olympia contest would be broadcast on American television for the first time, on ABC's *Wide World of Sports*. I would be photographed and painted by famous artists like Andy Warhol, Robert Mapplethorpe, Leroy Neiman, and Jamie Wyeth. In February 1976, Frank Zane, Ed Corney, and I were asked to pose for a group of art historians and art critics at the Whitney Museum in New York as part of an exhibit called "Articulate Muscle: The Male Body in Art" that *Sports Illustrated* described as a chance to look at us "not in athletic terms but as artists living inside our own creations." The event was so popular that the museum ran out of chairs and had to ask most of the audience to sit on the floor!

At the beginning of the decade, the idea that the "muscle-bound freaks" from this weird little subculture would be called artists or works of art, or that publications like the *Los Angeles Times* and *Sports Illustrated* would run legitimate news stories about us, would have seemed impossible to imagine. And yet, here we were. We'd arrived. By effectively turning myself into the front man for bodybuilding, I was able to help us finally present and explain the sport in a way that advanced the narrative toward things we were all trying to achieve.

By 1975 or 1976, bodybuilding had evolved from a subculture to part of culture. By the end of the decade, everyone from dancers to doctors was giving weight training a shot. People were lifting to look good and to feel good and for general fitness. They were using weights as part of physical therapy and rehabilitation. Athletes in other sports were lifting more, too, as a way to get a competitive edge. As a result, gyms started to pop up everywhere.

I think Joe was counting on all this happening. It's the other reason he paid for my ticket and set me up in those early days. He knew that I was the kind of hustler who was going to sell the shit out of bodybuilding in order to make my own dream come true, and in the process it would make his dream come true as well.

This is the critical distinction about what Joe Weider did that, if you appreciate it, can unlock the full potential of your vision. Through salesmanship, Joe made bodybuilding out to be more than it actually was, but then every decision he made and every step he took after that was geared toward turning those marketing promises into reality. What he did, as a dreamer and a marketer and a self-promoter, was project to the world where he knew bodybuilding and his own business could go if he continued to do what he was doing. He was showing anyone who had a similar dream what the road map and the destination were, and if you wanted to join him on his quest to make bodybuilding mainstream, you could be a big part of how it happened. That he hadn't gotten there yet wasn't a lie. It was only a matter of when, not if. Today, the fitness industry does $100 billion in revenue every year.

Joe was ahead of his time. Many of today's most famous entrepreneurs have followed in his footsteps even if they don't realize it, because his kind of promotion and selling is how successful Silicon Valley start-ups, like Airbnb, for example, charted a course to becoming global billion-dollar "unicorns." If instead of talking about the revolutionary potential for an average person to be able to spend the night in someone's home anywhere in the world, the company's founders had only talked about their original idea of being a hospitality alternative for people attending conferences in cities where all the hotel rooms were booked up, there's no way they'd have grown as big as they have. Even if the founders had said, "Hey, we're ready to grow beyond this idea and we're excited to see where it could lead!" nobody was going to bite if they weren't also articulating and selling the larger vision as if they were already halfway down that particular entrepreneurial path. This much I learned from Joe very early on.

There is a motivational saying I love: "See it. Believe it. Achieve it." But I think it's missing a step in between: *Explain it.* Before you can achieve your goals, I think you need to express them. Share them. I think you need to admit to yourself, and communicate to others, that this thing that started in your mind as a little idea has exploded into a massive dream with huge potential to benefit your life and theirs.

## LET THEM UNDERESTIMATE YOU

A good salesman knows that the key to making a sale and creating a customer for life is to give the customer more than they expected and leave them feeling like they're always getting the better end of the deal. When it's you that you're selling, the best way to exceed expectations every time is to keep those expectations low for as long as possible. Or maybe a better way to put it is that you shouldn't be afraid to let your customer hold on to their low expectations, because then it's that much easier for you to blow them away and sell them on what you have to offer.

Two weeks before the recall election in 2003, I took part in a televised debate with the four other major candidates. This was *the* high-stakes moment of that crazy campaign. Five hundred members of the media applied for credentials to attend. There were at least sixty cameras in the room. The debate was being broadcast live on all the national cable news channels, as well as on every local network affiliate around the state. According to polling from that week, two thirds of likely voters said the outcome of the debate would significantly impact who they voted for. The main Democratic candidate, Lieutenant Governor Cruz Bustamante, was in the lead going in. Nobody knew what to expect, but judging by the news stories leading up to the debate, everyone was expecting me to fall on my face.

For weeks, it was nothing but questions about my credibility. He's an actor, is he for real? He's a bodybuilder, does he have any ideas? Can he really be that smart? He's rich and famous, does he actually care? How can he possibly be qualified to lead forty million people and guide the world's sixth-largest economy?

I won't lie: to my ego, all these questions were fucking frustrating. I'd been dealing with this kind of doubt ever since I moved to America, at every stage, in every arena, for what I believe is the same reason each time: no one had ever seen someone like me before. In the 1970s, there weren't a lot of guys walking around Los Angeles carrying 235 pounds of muscle. In the '80s, Hollywood didn't have any action heroes who looked like they could *actually* kill bad guys. There were no leading men with muscles as thick as their accent either. I remember when I went on my first late-night talk show, I answered the simplest question, and the host said, "You can talk! Oh my God, ladies and gentlemen, he can talk!" And they all cheered. The same thing was happening again as I moved into politics.

If you ever find yourself in a similar position with people who hold positions of power or influence, and whom you have to sell your vision to, realize that they're handing you a golden opportunity. When you're different, when you're unique, and nobody has ever dealt with someone like you before, they are going to drastically underestimate what you're capable of.

Do not let your ego win. Don't correct them. If you can stay focused on winning and on achieving your goals, you can use their doubts and underestimation against them to effortlessly bridge the conversation, or the interview, or the negotiation to whatever you want to talk about.

Bridging is a communication technique that anyone can use to take control of a hostile discussion or to avoid a question you don't want to answer by shifting it toward a topic that better serves your agenda instead of the agenda of the person on the other side of the microphone or the negotiating table. I first learned about bridging from the late Jim Lorimer, my longtime friend, mentor, and business partner in the Arnold Sports Festival. Jim was an attorney, an FBI agent, a local politician, an executive at an insurance company, a law professor, and the author of multiple law textbooks. The man knew a thing or two about answering the question he wanted to answer, not the one you asked. Jim's point to me was that no one who puts a microphone in front of your face and asks you a bunch of question is doing it as a favor to you. They have their own agenda, whether that's finding a way to fill up column inches, coaxing out a controversial statement that gets more attention, or in some cases just trying to make you look like an asshole.

You don't owe them anything. You definitely don't owe them the answer they think they deserve. This is your time as much as it is theirs. This is your opportunity to tell your story and sell your vision as much as it is their opportunity to craft whatever narrative interests them. So take that time and opportunity to bridge the conversation from what they want to hear to what you need to say in order to achieve your goals.

The way you do this, Jim taught me, is to listen to the question being asked and then to start your response by accepting the premise of the question in order to establish common ground with your questioner. Once you've made them feel a little more comfortable by doing that, then you immediately pivot to reframe the question and say whatever you want. Here, I'll show you.

"Arnold, you've never run for office before at any level. What makes you think you're equipped to run the biggest state in the country?"

"That's a great question, but you know a better question is how can the greatest state in the country afford to continue down this road with the same kind of politicians who got us into this mess in the first place?"

It's like judo. You don't want to resist the momentum of the people who are underestimating you. Instead, you want to use their momentum against them by grabbing ahold of it then pivoting and tossing their asses out of the ring. You want to bridge their bullshit right into the garbage where it belongs.

Without knowing it, what critics and journalists had succeeded in doing with their condescending questions leading up to the debate was to make bridging to my agenda feel like a walk in the park. All they did with their simplistic stories about my candidacy was lower the bar for what voters needed to hear from me in order to buy me as a viable gubernatorial candidate. By the night of the debate, it felt like all I needed to do was show up sober and stay awake and I would have met the media's expectations for my performance.

I decided to do them one better. As the debate descended into chaos and candidates started sniping at one another from either side of this weirdly V-shaped dais, I focused on bridging every leading question by the moderator and every snarky comment from one of my opponents to talking about leadership, rattling off a few of my policy ideas, and then ripping off a few timely jokes for good measure. Arianna Huffington did not like it when I told her I had a part for her in *Terminator 4*. She liked it almost as much as Cruz Bustamante liked being called "Gray Davis: The Sequel." My goal over the course of the night was to show that I was a good listener, an effective communicator, a fighter, and a patriot who felt it was time to give back by putting Californians first. Basically, I wanted to show voters that I was the opposite of everyone and everything that led us to the recall in the first place.

I succeeded.

The day before the debate I had approximately 25 percent support in the polls. On Election Day just two weeks later, I got 48.6 percent of the vote—4.2 million votes in total. More than 300,000 votes better than the second and third place finishers *combined*.

People couldn't believe it. Media outlets across the country wrote stories after the election about my meteoric ascent. Except I hadn't ascended anywhere. I'd done hours of prep, I'd rehearsed the jokes I peppered in, I went over and over my talking points until I knew them cold, I had my arms fully around all the policies I felt were most important for the future of California. In short, I was right where I had always been. It was everybody else who finally got on my level by recognizing what they had been underestimating the whole time.

# BE YOURSELF, OWN THE STORY, REAP THE REWARDS

It was November 10, 2005. I'd been governor of California for two years, and I'd just had my ass handed to me in a special election that I had called against many people's advice, in order to present four policy ideas to the voters that I couldn't make headway on by working with the legislature. As I told the group of reporters assembled at the Capitol for this press conference right after the election, when there's something I want to do, something that I really believe in, I can be forceful and impatient.

It was a tough campaign. We spent a lot of money. We got into a lot of fights, publicly and privately. News coverage of these battles was not friendly. My approval rating sank to 33 percent by the end, lower than George W. Bush's in California, which is saying something. With my reelection campaign just around the corner, analysts predicted that in misreading the political landscape I had doomed the rest of my tenure as governor.

Californians had elected me to blow up the status quo and fight the special interests that controlled the Capitol. What they were telling me now, at the ballot box, was "Hey, Schnitzel, we sent you up there to do the work, not to bring the work to us." Speaking to California's thirty-five million residents through the reporters in the room and the TV cameras behind them, I made sure Californians knew that I had received their message loud and clear.

"I take full responsibility for this election," I said. "I take full responsibility for its failure. The buck stops with me."

My staff stood behind me. I'd spent the previous day with them debriefing, digging into returns, and getting a much better feel for the numbers. They were grim. Three of the four measures lost by double digits. This wasn't my team's fault, and I told the people just that. Before coming out to speak to the press, I'd spent hours in a closed-door breakfast meeting with the leadership of the Senate and the Assembly. On the menu was crow with a side of "I told you so," and I ate my share of both. When I announced the election five months earlier, this was not how I envisioned stepping up to the microphone to take responsibility for its outcome.

Put yourself in my shoes for a minute. What do you think that must have felt like? Standing up in front of my adversaries as well as the people who believed in me most, in front of the entire state, the entire country, really, and admitting that I'd gotten it wrong. That I'd made a mistake. I'd upset a lot of people, and it was my fault, nobody else's.

You might be surprised, but it wasn't actually difficult at all. Sure, taking responsibility for the outcome of an entire election—and its very existence, if we're being honest— was unique for a high-profile politician. But it wasn't unique for me. I don't shy away from responsibility. I own who I am and the things I do—my successes and my failures. This was just the most recent example of being confronted with a controversial decision or an uncomfortable truth and owning it. During the recall campaign, I got questioned about past marijuana use. Unlike some other politicians, I didn't dodge around. I said, "Yes, and I did inhale." When some journalist dug up a wild video I'd done for *Playboy* during Carnival back in the early 1980s, I didn't try to explain it away or deny it. I simply said, "That was such a great time." Because it was.

Why lie? What is the point of that? One of the main

reasons people voted for me was that I'm *not* a typical politician with a phony flawless exterior. I'm a normal person who likes to do fun things. Why pretend that the things that got me where I was and made me who I am didn't happen? All I'd be doing is putting myself in a position to sell the story of someone I don't know.

This is something you should think about. What is the value of trying to be someone you're not? Of hiding from your true story and letting someone else tell it? Where do you think that gets you in the end? I promise you, it's nowhere good. Embrace who you are! Own your story! Even if you don't like it. Even if it's bad, and you're ashamed. If you run away and hide from your past, if you deny your story and try to sell a different one, even if you mean well, it just makes you seem like a con artist. Or worse, a politician.

In that light, taking responsibility for the election was an easy choice. Also, it was the right and smart thing to do if I still wanted to achieve the vision I had for California when I first decided to run for governor. If I didn't stand up and explain what happened, why it happened, who was responsible, how things would be different, and where we would go from there—if I didn't fill this bucket first—then my opponents and all those journalists standing in front of me were going to explain it themselves, in their own ways, twisting my ideas and using the words of other people whose vision was probably not aligned with mine.

So what exactly did happen? Ironically, I failed to tell the story well. I failed to sell the value proposition of each measure I'd put on the ballot, and I failed to connect them well enough to my vision for California. I failed to effectively communicate the issues at the heart of each ballot measure. Why had I failed? I was too aggressive with my rhetoric. I was too technical with my explanations. I assumed people would know what I was talking about, or that they would learn, because these issues were important and seriously impacted their lives.

Boy, had I lost sight of who my customers were. The moderate and undecided voters I needed to persuade didn't see at all how these issues connected to their lives. Teacher tenure. State spending limits. Union dues and political contributions. Even redistricting reform failed to connect with them. In that case, it was because I made it about the mechanics of redrawing district boundaries instead of the philosophy behind why we were trying to change them in the first place: to get the power out of the hands of the politicians so the state's districts would more accurately reflect how people lived.

Simply put, I'd filled the bucket with a bunch of shit that most Californians weren't interested in wading through at the time. It was my fault, and I wasn't going to do that to the people ever again. Nor would I make them settle disputes that arose between my office and the legislature. Going forward we would figure out what things we could work together on, then we'd focus on passing legislation in those areas. This was the promise I made to the people at the press conference, and that is exactly what happened.

Don't believe me? Let me tell you how the next few years went. Over the next year, the legislature and I worked together like never before. We had amazing, constructive sessions that resulted in Assembly Bill (AB) 32, a landmark environmental bill that aimed to reduce greenhouse gas emissions by 25 percent by 2020; Senate Bill (SB) 1, the most ambitious solar energy policy ever attempted, which came to be known as the "million solar roofs" initiative; and a $50 billion infrastructure package to rebuild California's roads, highways, bridges, classrooms, levees, affordable housing, and rail systems, among other things. And you know what the key was to selling that infrastructure package to the people? Having learned my lesson from 2005, I rarely ever used technical words like "infrastructure" by themselves. Instead I talked about needing to fix our old roads and build new ones so parents wouldn't be stuck in traffic for so long and miss their kids' soccer practices so often. I talked about fixing bridges and railroad lines so that people could buy the things they needed when they needed them. The faster we moved people and goods around, I told California voters, the more that increased our economic power. I stopped talking about the corruption and inequities of our state's redistricting policies, and instead explained to voters that I wanted to take the power away from the politicians and give it to the people. I told my story using language that actually connected to the lives of the people who I was trying to sell. Then, in June 2006, I was reelected governor with an even greater share of the vote (55.9 percent) and even more total votes (4.85 million) than in 2003.

Just imagine if I hadn't called that postelection press conference. If, instead, I'd retreated to my office and refused to talk to anyone or to issue any comment. Refusing to take responsibility for my fuckup and apologize would have made me a typical politician, which was exactly the opposite of what voters said they wanted when they elected me. But even worse, it would have given every single media outlet reporting on the election carte blanche to fill the bucket for the public with their own version of events. Without a doubt, the stories would have been horrific. The narrative would have been, "It only took Arnold two years to become part of the problem— another heartless, arrogant, out-of-touch politician." I can see the snarky headlines: ARNOLD GETS TERMINATED BY VOTERS. LAST ACTION ZERO. HASTA LA VISTA, GOVERNATOR.

Except none of those headlines happened. The news stories that followed were nothing like the stories about the 2003 gubernatorial debate and the recall election. There was no sense of shock or surprise. They weren't full of gossip or bogus lines. If anything, the stories in 2005 were boring. Matter-of-fact. Almost uninteresting. They were typical political analysis and commentary. Because I had made a choice, just as you have a choice, to own my story, to write it myself, in my own words.

In those first two days after the special election, the analysts who were predicting my downfall considered it unthinkable that the Democratic-controlled legislature would even entertain working with what everyone as-sumed was now a lame-duck Republican governor. That I would be reelected in a landslide less than eight months later . . . that probably sounded like the plot of a science-fiction movie. It turned out to be a true story.

Nothing sells better than a true story from a genuine person. Especially when the story is about that person. This doesn't just relate to getting elected or getting featured in a magazine. It's the same if you're trying to get a raise from your boss, the attention of someone you're interested in, or the blessing of your family as you enlist in the military. In every case, no matter what your dream is, you are selling yourself, and you're selling the story of the life you're trying to create for yourself. Either you fill that bucket openly and honestly in your own words or someone else does it for you and reaps the rewards at your expense.

It might sound scary right now, but you can do it, I promise you. I've been around a long time. I've met a lot of happy, successful people from all over the world. Famous people. Powerful people. Interesting, creative people. Normal, good, hardworking people. What they all have in common is that they never let anyone else write their stories. They know how to sell their vision better than anyone, and they walk peacefully through the world confident in that knowledge.

# CHAPTER 5

# SHIFT GEARS

I n March 2020, I was stuck at home like most people, glued to my television watching the news about the deadly virus that was sweeping across the globe and had just shut down most of the country here in America. Over and over in those early days of the pandemic, all we were hearing from the president of the United States and the governor of California, where I live, was that we didn't have enough ventilators or masks and other personal protective equipment (PPE) for hospital staff and first responders. We had some stuff in strategic reserves, they were telling us, but that would be gone in no time and it could take weeks, maybe even months, to secure enough PPE to satisfy the growing need. There was no timetable at all for ventilators.

I couldn't believe what I was hearing. This was insanity to me. The United States is the third largest country in the world by population and the biggest economy in the world. What do you mean we can't get enough masks? There's no way.

I called a handful of hospitals around Los Angeles I'd had interactions with over the years, either as a patient or a politician. I called UCLA Medical Center, Cedars-Sinai, Martin Luther King Jr. Community Hospital, Kech Hospital of USC, and Santa Monica Medical Center. I asked the administrators at each place how things were looking. All of them were having a hell of a time getting PPE. A few of the hospitals were already having their doctors and nurses take their masks home at night to wash and then reuse on their next shift. The other hospitals were almost at that point, but they were hoping the state would come through before they got there.

This was really frustrating to me. Back in 2006, during an outbreak of avian flu in Asia, I allocated more than $200 million to building out a strategic reserve of medical supplies and equipment for the state of California, called the Health Surge Capacity Initiative, in case of a pandemic just like this. It contained fifty million N95 masks and nearly twenty-five hundred ventilators, along with all the equipment you'd need to build out football field–sized mobile hospitals, and the funding necessary to maintain the stockpile. But then five years later, during a budget crunch, my successor stopped funding the stockpile in order to save a few million bucks a year. Eventually, all the masks and ventilators became unusable, even the ones given to local hospitals, because no one was given additional money to maintain them.

This early into the pandemic, our strategic reserve would easily have had all these hospitals covered. And now here we were, with hospital administrators in the second largest city in the country looking to the leadership of the country's biggest state, who were looking to the leadership of the richest country in the history of the world—and no one had the first fucking idea what to do. No wonder people hate politicians. Hadn't any of them heard of the open market? Go on Alibaba.com and order ten million masks from a bunch of factories in China, I thought to myself. Or call one of those massive logistics companies whose entire business is sourcing stuff like masks in bulk and shipping them all over the world.

The incompetence drove me absolutely nuts. Still, I didn't say anything publicly or call out any of these leaders. For one, I'd been in their shoes, and I knew that crisis situations where solutions seem obvious from the outside are always more complicated than they look. But more importantly, I have a rule: no complaining about a situation unless you're prepared to do something to make it better. If you see a problem and you don't come to the table with a potential solution, I don't want to hear your whining about how bad it is. It couldn't be that bad if it hasn't motivated you to try to fix it.

And when exactly has complaining ever gotten someone closer to achieving their goals? You work to make a dream come true, you don't whine it into existence. Plus, problems and adversity are a normal part of every person's journey. Whatever your vision is, there is going to be struggle. Tough times. Things that bug the shit out of you. You have to learn how to manage those moments. You have to get good at shifting gears and finding the positive in things. You have to know how to reframe the failure you experience and understand the risks you're undertaking. Confronting problems instead of complaining about them gives you the chance to practice all these skills.

In my case, with the mask shortage, I realized that shifting gears—from bitching to Lulu and Whiskey (my donkey and my miniature horse) while I watched the news out on my patio, to solving the problem that these jackass politicians had created—would actually give me an opportunity to execute on my vision for this phase of my life, which is helping as many people as possible.

I called my chief of staff. His wife worked for one of those logistics companies I just mentioned. "Call her," I said, "see if there's something we can do to help these people."

We got someone on the phone that afternoon, and, wouldn't you know it, the logistics company, Flexport, was already working with someone who was trying to solve this problem as part of a fundraising campaign called the Frontline Responders Fund. They'd put some money in, the Flexport representative told us, but if we wanted to join them that would be fantastic, because they had a line on millions of masks and other forms of PPE in China that were headed stateside. The only question was how many millions we were going to buy.

My first thought was, How does the president or the governor or our senators, or *any* senators, not know about this? You'd think they'd at least want to pretend they had their heads in the game instead of up their asses. But I caught myself. There was no time for complaining. I couldn't risk letting my frustration with the failure of the system get in the way of helping to find a solution to this problem.

My next thought was, How quickly can I get a million dollars to these people? And then, How quickly can we get masks to each of the local hospitals I'd been in contact with? Flexport said they'd be on the ground in the United States in three days, and crates of PPE would be earmarked for each hospital. I immediately called my office and told them to send a million dollars to the Frontline Responders Fund that day. By the end of the week, those crates filled with hundreds of thousands of masks each were on their way to hospitals.

# SHIFT GEARS AND FIND THE POSITIVE

Only fairly recently have social scientists really understood why we seem to respond to negative things more strongly than we do to positive things. We click on negative images and news stories more than positive ones. We focus more energy worrying about negative outcomes than hoping for positive results. We even have more words to describe our negative emotions than we do for our positive emotions. There's a name for this phenomenon: it's called "negativity bias," and scientists tell us that it's probably a kind of survival mechanism. Our ancestors who worried less about what could make them sick or kill them and focused more on pleasant experiences probably tended to get weeded out disproportionately, so over the last six million years of human evolution we have geared ourselves to be more sensitive to negative influences than to positive ones. We have many biases from our deep past that aren't as useful as they once were, and this is no doubt one of them.

It makes a lot of sense when you think about it, but I'll be honest with you: I have no use for any of it in my life. To me, focusing on all that negativity is a waste of time, because I don't just want to survive, I want to thrive, and I want you to thrive too. That's why I believe we all have to get better at embracing our circumstances and shifting our perspective toward finding the positive in whatever situation we find ourselves in.

I know this is harder for some than others. I'm fortunate; I've always been this way, for as long as I can remember. All my friends will tell you that one of the most distinctive things about me is my ability to find joy in everything I do. Being positive has made my life better, it's that simple. I know it can make your life better too. Hell, it might even save it one day. Talk to any good oncologist and they will tell you that if you show them a patient with a positive attitude, they will show you a patient with a positive prognosis. It sounds a little bit like fairy-tale thinking, I know, but what cancer doctors know better than anyone is that if you feel powerless to affect your circumstances, you're right. If you believe that you can triumph over them—not just survive in spite of them but actually thrive *because* of them—then you are also right.

I think a lot about how different my life could have been if I wasn't a positive person, if I'd responded differently to my upbringing in Thal. I didn't have a hot shower or regular meat in my diet until l left for the army as a teenager. My daily morning routine involved fetching water and chopping firewood, which was brutal in the wintertime and earned me exactly zero sympathy from my father, who'd been through much worse when he was a kid. There were no free passes in Gustav Schwarzenegger's house. No free meals either. I had to do two hundred knee bends every morning just to "earn" my breakfast. Nothing works up an appetite like bobbing up and down like a pogo stick on an empty stomach.

The drudgery of all that discomfort and thankless labor could have broken my spirit or made the images of America that I saw in magazines and newsreels seem impossibly far away. It could have drubbed the instinct to look over the horizon out of me. I certainly wasn't getting any encouragement at home to think about life beyond the hills of southeastern Austria. There was a good job with the police waiting for me when I got out of the army. Others should be so lucky, my father thought. He also didn't understand or approve of my interest in bodybuilding. He thought it was egotistical and selfish. "Why don't you chop some wood instead," he would say, "you can get big and strong that way and at least then you will have done something for somebody else." Then there were the times he would come home drunk after work and hit us. Those nights were very hard.

I could very easily have allowed myself to get wrapped up in all that, but I chose to look at the positive. I have always made that choice—to recognize that on the vast majority of days my father was a good dad and my mother was the best mom. That life wasn't exciting or particularly comfortable, not by modern standards anyway, but it was a good life. A life where I learned a lot and I found my passion, my purpose, and my first mentors.

Even with the undeniably bad things, I choose to re-member that they were a big part of what drove me to es-cape, to achieve, to become the person I am today. If my childhood was just a little bit better, you might not be holding this book right now. And if it was a little bit worse, you might not be holding it either, because I could have fallen down the same rabbit hole of alcoholism that my brother fell down, which eventually cost him his life in a drunk-driving accident in 1971.

I owe a lot to my upbringing. I was made for it and made by it. I wouldn't be who I am today without each one of those experiences. The Stoics have a term for this: *amor fati.* Love of fate. "Do not seek for things to happen the way you want them to," the great Stoic philosopher and former slave Epictetus said. "Rather, wish that what hap-pens happen the way it happens. Then you will be happy."

Nietzsche talks about this too. He says, "My formula for greatness in a human being is amor fati: that one wants nothing to be different, not forward, not backward, not in all eternity. Not merely bear what is necessary . . . but love it."

To get to this place takes some work. It's not intuitive to stare adversity or unpleasantness in the face and think, "Yes, this is what I needed. This is what I *wanted.* I love this." Ironically, our natural negativity bias draws us toward all the bad stuff happening out in the world, but it makes us want to run away, to deny, to turn a blind eye to difficulty when it finds its way to our doorstep. And if that doesn't work, then we just complain about it. It happens to the best of us. We're all guilty of it, all the time, with big things just as often as with little things.

Anytime I find myself in a shitty situation and I feel that urge to bitch and moan rising up within me, I stop, take a breath, and tell myself that it's time to switch gears. I will actually talk to myself out loud and remind myself to look for the positive in my situation.

In March 2018, I found myself in one of the shittiest situations possible: the postoperative intensive care unit after what was supposed to be a "minimally invasive" valve-replacement procedure turned into full-blown open-heart surgery. At some point during the operation, the surgeon accidentally blew through my heart wall, so they had to quickly crack my chest open and repair the damage while they replaced the valve the old-fashioned way.

Had things gone normally, I would have been out of the hospital in a couple of days, then up and around like nothing had happened a couple of days after that. That was the whole reason I decided to have the procedure when I did. A few weeks before, I'd been in a meeting with a ninety-year-old man who'd had the same procedure only a few days before and he looked like he'd just been to a spa. This would be perfect timing, I thought. I knew I needed to replace the valve, which had a life span of ten to twelve years. It had originally been inserted in 1997, when I went in for my first heart surgery to fix what is called a bicuspid aortic valve, which is a kind of prenatal heart defect that can have no symptoms for some people their whole lives but can be fatal for others, like it would be for my mother the very next year. I'd been putting the replacement surgery off because I was busy and because last I'd heard heart surgery was still a bitch. Now I was being told that it was almost like arthroscopic surgery, which is exactly what I needed, because in a few months I had to be in Budapest to begin filming on *Terminator: Dark Fate*. The plan was to knock out the surgery, rest for a week, then get back into the gym to prepare for filming.

Then I woke up. The doctor was standing over me and a breathing tube was jammed down my throat. "I'm sorry, Arnold," the doctor said, "there were complications. We had to open you up."

As the doctor explained the situation, I had many thoughts and emotions spinning inside my head. I was scared, because they'd nearly killed me. I was pissed off, because this was going to be a major problem for production. I was frustrated, because I remembered what it took to get back to 100 percent after my first open-heart surgery, and I was twenty-one years younger then. It was also a little depressing when the doctors told me that I'd be in the hospital for at least a week, and I couldn't do any kind of lifting for at least a month once I was discharged. And they wouldn't let me leave until I could take deep breaths without aggravating my lungs, walk unassisted, and take a shit—or, as I called it, "declaring victory"— without help getting into and out of the bathroom.

I let all those emotions have their moment in my mind, but then when the doctors finally left the room, I said to myself, "OK, Arnold, this isn't what you would have preferred, but you're alive. Let's switch gears here. Now you have a goal, to get out of this place. And you have a mission, to do all your exercises and achieve the results that will get you discharged. It's time to get to work."

I rang the call button next to my bed. A nurse came in and I asked her to erase a section of the dry erase board on the wall across from me and to write the words "Breathing" and "Walking" at the top with a line underneath them. Every time I completed a session of the breathing exercises, or I did some walking and reached my target destination—the end of the hall, around the nurses' station, to the elevators—I asked her to add a tally mark to the board. I was going to treat this just like my old workouts back in Graz, and my preparation process for movies and speeches. This was a system that worked. I knew how to do this. Plus, it allowed me to track my progress visually, which gave me confidence and built momentum. It also meant I didn't have to think about it, so I could use all that mental energy to ignore the burning in my lungs as I inhaled and exhaled into a breathing apparatus that looked like a cross between a chemistry beaker and a cat toy. Not having to guess whether I was making progress allowed me to focus on firing my leg and arm and back muscles as I walked down the hospital corridors, first with a walker, then with a cane, and eventually just with the rolling IV stand that carried the bag connected to the drainage tube sticking out of my chest.

I "declared victory" a day earlier than expected, and I was home after just six days in the ICU. A month after the surgery—maybe a day or two earlier, if I'm being honest— I was in my home gym, with the IV stand next to me and the drainage tube still sticking out of my chest draped over the bar of the lat pulldown machine while I did a bunch of reps with no weight to wake my muscles up. Within another month, I was adding weight to every lift—twenty pounds, then forty, then sixty, and so on. A month after that, I was on a plane to Budapest to begin filming, right on schedule.

I don't tell this story very often, but when I do, a lot of people ask me if I sued the doctors for nearly killing me on the table. This always surprises me, because never once did I think about it. Mistakes happen. In fact, I knew beforehand that mistakes can happen with this kind of procedure. The actor Bill Paxton died from complications during a similar valve-replacement procedure at the same hospital the year prior. It's why I told the hospital administrators that I wouldn't do the operation there unless the open-heart surgery team was in the room during my procedure. Beyond that, and beyond the fact that I'd prepared for this possibility, these doctors are only human. They did the best they could. And don't forget, they saved my life! What would be the point of suing them? It doesn't change what happened. Who would benefit besides the lawyers? What positive thing could any of us take from that experience if it ended in a lawsuit?

The famous Austrian psychologist and Holocaust survivor Viktor Frankl said, "You cannot control what happens to you in life, but you can always control what you will feel and do about what happens to you." So here are some questions for you: How many hours do you think you waste every week complaining about things that happened to you that are out of your control? How much time do you spend worrying about things that might happen that you couldn't possibly predict or prevent? How many minutes a day do you allow yourself to read articles and social media posts that piss you off but have nothing to do with your life? How many times have you gotten angry in traffic and carried that negative emotion with you into the office, or the classroom, or through your front door at home? We just talked about how full your daily schedule is and how you need to protect those precious few hours you have every week to do the work of achieving your vision. By giving into negativity, you're allowing these things to steal time from you, from your dream, and from the people closest to you whom it's your job to lead—whether it's your family, your intramural sports team, your project group at work, your unit, whatever it is.

But you can take back that time! You can repurpose it. You can make it productive. You can turn a negative situation into a positive experience. It all starts by catching yourself any time you start to complain, then talking yourself into switching gears and looking for the good in things. If you can choose joy over jealousy, happiness over hate, love over resentment, positivity over negativity, then you have the tools to make the best of any situation, even one that feels like failure.

# REFRAME FAILURE

People come up to me all the time and say, "Arnold, I didn't hit the goal I set for myself, what should I do?" Or they say, "Arnold, I asked out my crush and they said no." Or "I failed this week to get the promotion I wanted, what do I do now?"

My answer to them is simple: Learn from your mistakes and then say, "I'll be back."

Often, that's all the advice people need. They're just a little scared, or maybe a little desperate, and they need some encouragement to get back on track. But then there are the others, who want to complain that life is unfair because this thing they wanted so badly didn't happen exactly when they wanted it to, and it hurts too much to think about the possibility that maybe they didn't do enough of the work to achieve their desired outcome.

I don't say this with any judgment; I've been there. When I lost to Frank Zane in 1968, I was despondent and inconsolable. I cried in my hotel room all night afterward. It felt like the world had come crashing down on me. I questioned what I was even doing coming to America. I was away from my parents, I was away from my friends, I didn't speak the language, I didn't know anyone in Miami. I was all alone. And for what? For second place to a guy who was smaller than me?

I blamed everyone and everything else for my loss. The judging was unfair. The judges were biased toward Frank, who was an American. Traveling from London and eating crappy food in the airport days before had affected my body and training negatively. The loss was too painful for me to look in the mirror and admit that maybe I hadn't done enough to win, that it was my fault.

The next morning at breakfast, Joe Weider invited me to come out to Los Angeles. It was only after working out with the guys at Gold's over the next few weeks that I was finally able to see the difference between Frank and me, and to admit that he'd won fair and square. I simply wasn't as well-defined. This was true not just in comparison to Frank, but in comparison to almost all the American guys I was working out with. I was bigger than them, and I had better symmetry, but they were doing something I wasn't doing that was allowing them to get very cut. If I wanted to be the best, I had to figure out what that was and start doing it myself. So once I got settled in my new apartment in Santa Monica, I invited Frank to come stay with me so we could train together and he could show me a thing or two. To his credit, he accepted my invitation. He stayed with me for a month, we worked out at Gold's together every day, he showed me the exercises he did to get completely shredded, and then he never beat me again.

Let me be very clear about something. And this is for anyone out there who has ever experienced failure, which is every single one of us: failure is not fatal. I know, I know, that's such a cliché. But all positive talk about failure has become a cliché at this point, because we all know it's the truth. Everyone who has accomplished something they're proud of, who we admire as a society, will tell you that they learned more from their failures than from their successes. They will tell you that failure isn't the end. And they're right.

If anything, when you look at it with the right perspective, failure is actually the beginning of measurable success, because failure is only possible in situations where you've tried to accomplish something difficult and worthwhile. You can't fail when you don't try. In that sense, failure is kind of like a progress report on your path to purpose. It shows you how far you've come, and it reminds you how far you still have to go and what you have to work on to get there. It's an opportunity to learn from your mistakes, to evolve your approach, and to come back better than ever.

I first learned this, like I learned many things, in the gym training for weight-lifting competitions when I was younger. The beauty of weight lifting is that failure is baked into the practice. The whole goal in weight lifting is to work your muscles to failure, which we sometimes forget. When you can't squeeze out that last rep or lock out those elbows before dropping the weight, it's not uncommon to feel a flash of frustration, but then you have to remember that your failure on that particular lift doesn't mean you've lost somehow. It actually means that your workout was a good one, that your muscles were fully fatigued. It means you did the work.

In the gym, failure doesn't equal defeat, it equals success. It's one of the reasons I've always been comfortable pushing the limits in everything I do. When failure is a positive part of the game you play, it's much less scary to search for the limits of your ability—whether that's speaking English, acting in big movies, or tackling big social problems—and then once you've found those limits, to grow beyond them. The only way to do that, though, is to constantly test yourself in a manner that risks repeated failure.

This is how weight-lifting competitions are designed. In a traditional meet, you get three lifts. Your first lift is a sure thing. It's a weight you've done before and you're comfortable with. The purpose is to get your feet underneath you, to get the butterflies out, and to make sure you've put one good lift on the board. Your second lift is a little bit of a stretch: you lift something at or near your personal record weight, with the goal of putting some pressure on your competitors. Maybe you don't win in the end, but at least you can leave knowing that you'd hit your previous max. On your third lift, you are trying to lift a weight you have never lifted before. You are trying to break new ground—for yourself as a weight lifter and for the state of the sport itself. This final lift is where records are broken and victories are won. It's also where failure quite often occurs. As a weight lifter, I failed on ten different final lifts to bench press 500 pounds, back when that figure was almost unheard of. Once I finally did it, benching 500 pounds got easier and set me on a course to eventually put up 525 pounds.

That third lift is a microcosm for chasing your dreams out in the real world. It will be hard, and it will feel unfamiliar. People will be watching and judging, and failure is a real possibility. Failure is inevitable in a lot of ways. But when it comes to achieving your vision, it isn't failure you have to worry about, it's giving up. Failure has never killed a dream; quitting kills every dream it touches. No one who has set a world record, or started a successful business, or set the high score on a video game, or done anything difficult at all that they cared about, has been a quitter. They got to where they are on the back of numerous failures. They reached the pinnacle of their profession, invented world-changing products, achieved their craziest visions because they persevered through failure and actively paid attention to the lessons that failure is designed to teach us.

Take someone like the chemist who invented the lubricant spray WD-40. The full name of WD-40 is "Water Displacement, 40th Formula." It was called that in the chemist's lab book because his previous thirty-nine versions of the formula failed. He learned from each one of those failures and nailed it on the fortieth try.

Thomas Edison is legendary for learning from his failures. So much so that he refused to even call them failures. In the 1890s, for example, Edison and his team were trying to develop a nickel-iron battery. Over the course of about six months, they created more than nine thousand prototypes that all failed. When one of his assistants commented that it was a shame they hadn't produced any promising results, Edison said, "Why, man, I have gotten a lot of results! I know several thousand things that won't work." This was how Edison looked at the world—as a scientist, an inventor, and a businessman. It was this kind of positive mindset, this sort of brilliant reframing of failure, that led Edison to the invention of the lightbulb barely a decade earlier and to the thousand other patents issued to him by the time he died.

As you think about this thing you want to do, or the mark you want to make in this world, remember that your job is neither to avoid failure nor to seek it out. Your job is to bust your ass in pursuit of your vision—yours and nobody else's—and to embrace the failure that is bound to come. Much like how those last painful reps in the gym are a signal that you're one step closer to your goal, failure is a signal of which direction your next step should go. Or like Edison would say, which direction it shouldn't go. This is why failure is worth the risk and important to embrace: it teaches you what doesn't work and points you toward the things that do.

Personally, I attribute a number of my successes as governor, including my reelection, to having learned from the failure of the 2005 special election and then using those lessons as a guide for what to do next. The voters told me that bringing my disagreements with the legislature to their doorstep was a huge mistake. They told me that speaking like a technocrat or a policy wonk, instead of like the normal person and the non-politician they'd elected, wasn't going to work for them. If I wanted to get anything done, Californians were saying, I definitely couldn't take those approaches again. With their votes, they were asking instead for explanations in plain English, and they were pointing me in the direction of my adversaries, telling me that the solution to my problem was there.

So I listened to them. After the election, I invited the leadership of both parties, from both houses of the legislature, on my plane, and we flew to Washington, DC, to meet with California's entire congressional delegation and talk about ways to better serve the people. For five hours in each direction, we sat together in close quarters, forty thousand feet over America, and talked not as political opponents but as public servants with a common cause: helping California's residents live happier, richer, healthier lives. By the time we got home a few days later, the broad strokes of a number of bipartisan initiatives had been sketched out.

Had I ignored the lessons from 2005, had I chosen to whine about the outcome of the special election, had I vilified my opponents instead of defying political convention and taking responsibility for my policy failures, there's very little chance that any of this stuff gets done and there's no chance in hell that I get reelected a year later. It's not an exaggeration to say that these successes I was fortunate enough to enjoy were the direct result of learning from failure.

## BREAK THE RULES

In 1972, the comedian George Carlin released a comedy album called *Class Clown*, with a bit that would become one of the most famous of all time. Called "Seven Words You Can Never Say on Television," it's a long riff on the seven dirty words you couldn't say on American airwaves.

In the Schwarzenegger house, we have our own seven dirty words: "It's how things have always been done." When I hear those words, I see red. It bothers me when people use them to justify saying no to new things that they don't understand. But what really pisses me off is when the people who are doing the new things being objected to accept that seven-word status quo and give up. That makes me want to go full "John Matrix in the toolshed."

When you're chasing a big vision, you have to expect that you'll face resistance. People who lack vision are threatened by those who have it. Their instinct is to throw their hands up and say, "No! Wait a minute, let's slow down here." It's not that they think you can't do it, like the typical naysayer, it's that they think it shouldn't be done in the first place. New ideas are scary to them. Big projects are intimidating. They're uncomfortable around people who want to break the mold or make waves. For whatever reason, they're much more at ease with people who can accept without questioning that there is simply a way things have always been done.

I am not one of those people, obviously. My guess is that you're not one of those people either. My entire life has been an exercise in doing things differently than they've always been done. As a bodybuilder, I did two full workouts a day, not one like everybody else. As an actor, I didn't do bit parts in TV shows or films, like producers said I should; I went after starring roles only. As a politician, I didn't run for city council or mayor or state senator, like the party bosses and the kingmakers said I had to; I went right after the governorship. My vision from the very beginning was to be the best bodybuilder, then the biggest star, then to help the most people. Not *someday*, not eventually, but as soon as I possibly could. There was no room in my plan for paying dues or climbing some invisible ladder or waiting for permission.

That didn't sit very well with the gatekeepers, power brokers, and status quo minders who I came up against in each of these phases of my life. The only thing that bothered them more than my willingness to make waves was the fact that I didn't listen to their complaints, and I didn't care that it bothered them.

This was never more the case than during my tenure as governor. I broke a lot of rules while I was in Sacramento, and no one got more upset than the people in my own party. When I hired Susan Kennedy, a Democrat, as my chief of staff, they acted like I'd just let the fox into the henhouse. One Republican lawmaker was so concerned, he came into my office, sat down on the sofa next to my chair, looked around the room like some kind of conspiratorial cartoon villain, then whispered in my ear that she was a lesbian, in case I wasn't aware. Like a warning. I already knew that, of course, but what did that matter?

"But did you know she burned her bra!?" he said, clearly desperate to get me to change my mind.

"So?" I said. "I didn't need it."

And that was nothing compared to the reaction of Republican insiders when half my judicial appointments were Democrats. You would have thought that I'd desecrated Abraham Lincoln's grave while cursing Ronald Reagan's name. Appointing judges is one of those areas in politics where most politicians, whether they're a governor or the president, pick judges from their own party almost without exception. I told my people we weren't going to do that. I told them to send me the best possible candidates and remove their party affiliation from the briefing documents. Why? Because I promised voters that I would be a different kind of public servant, not the same old kind of party servant, and that meant picking the best people for the job. The result was half Democrats, half Republicans. Seems pretty fair and representative to me.

I told this story in 2012, during my speech at the opening of the USC Schwarzenegger Institute—a think tank dedicated to bipartisanship and putting people over politics, whose entire mission is basically to ignore the status quo and break the rules. I described to the audience how party hacks in Sacramento couldn't understand my thinking, and they couldn't stand that I ignored them. Then I explained that if there was one thing I had learned from both campaigning and governing, it was that the old way of doing things didn't work. The way things had always been done . . . it wasn't getting anything done anymore. The status quo wasn't serving the people well (it's why the people had elected me to begin with), and because my mission was to serve *all the people* as best as I could, I happily broke the rules that were standing in the way of my vision for progress and change and a better California.

That didn't make my job easier, politically speaking, but my mindset after the special election was to stop worrying about the status quo and to ignore the people obsessed with how things have always been done. Instead,

I focused on building working relationships with the people—in Sacramento and Washington and around the world, in some cases—who were just as sick of the old rules as I was and were more interested in getting things done. To everybody else, I said get on board or get out of the way, and if you do neither, expect to get worked around or run over.

Is there a risk in taking that kind of approach to achieving your ultimate vision? Possibly. But this is your life and these are your dreams we're talking about, not theirs. I would argue that doing whatever you need to do to make your dreams a reality and to create the life you want for yourself is worth the risk.

## RISK IS RELATIVE

If you're someone who is afraid of risk—which I understand, believe me—it might help to reframe risk the way we have reframed failure. Risk, in my opinion, isn't real. It's not something you can hold on to or count on. No two people have the same definition for it. It's a moving target. It's made up. A perception.

Risk is just the name we give to the conclusion that each one of us comes to independently when we evaluate a choice for its chances of success compared to the consequences of its failure. If you believe that something is highly unlikely to succeed and that the consequences for failure are hugely negative, then you will probably conclude that the choice is pretty risky. If the opposite is true—that success is likely and failure wouldn't be very costly—then the choice probably doesn't seem risky at all. Except it's not so cut-and-dried, because there is the upside of success to consider. If the upside isn't big enough, sometimes even a little bit of risk isn't worth it. But when it is big enough, like it often is with our dreams, then even something that you know is technically very risky can be worth the gamble. The reality is, when you want something bad enough, and it means enough to you, at some point you have to be willing to reach for the brass ring and not give a fuck about risk anymore. You have to embrace that sometimes the cliché is true: the bigger the risk, the bigger the reward.

Look at someone like the rock climber Alex Honnold. When he made the first ever free solo ascent of El Capitan in Yosemite National Park in 2017, many people thought he was completely insane. They thought he had a death wish. But then, after the documentary about his climb came out a year later and it won the Oscar, and he became famous and got a bunch of endorsement deals, all of a sudden you didn't hear so many people talking about how crazy he was. Before the fame and the money, he was a daredevil with a screw loose. After the fame and the money, he was a thoughtful, experienced climber. A hard-working professional who traveled the world and got paid to be outside in nature. He wasn't a bad influence anymore, he was an inspiration!

Of course, that's never how Honnold saw it, that's how *other people* saw it. After watching the documentary and reading interviews with him, their perception of his chances for success changed drastically and their opinions about the consequences of failure (which were injury or death) were muted by seeing what the upside of success looked like. He was the same guy that he was before any of us had heard his name; the only thing that changed was how much we knew about him.

The irony is, while our perception of the riskiness of his climbing has gone down, his perception of it has probably gone up. Not because the likelihood of a climb succeeding has decreased (if anything it's increased with experience), but because the negative consequences of failure have increased for him. Beyond simple injury or death, which were always present during his free solo attempts, he now has a wife and daughter who love him and a foundation that relies on him. He now has more to lose.

That, to me, has always been the real question when it comes to thinking about risk: What do you have to lose? The reason my risk tolerance has always been very high, and therefore why I've done so many things that people thought were unlikely or impossible, is because for most of my early life I didn't have a lot to lose. And as I got older and more successful, and I started doing new things, I knew how to minimize my downside in case I failed.

When you consider how I grew up, what did I have to lose spending all those hours in the gym in Graz working on my body and then moving to Munich to work for a stranger in his gym before finally coming to America?

What did I have to lose going into acting? If I stunk at it and nobody wanted to give me another shot, I still would have been a seven-time Mr. Olympia. I still would have had Joe Weider in my corner and my training booklets to sell and my apartment building to give me a roof over my head.

What did I have to lose going into politics? If I lost the

recall election, even if I performed poorly in the televised debate and embarrassed myself, I would still have been a movie star with lots of hobbies. I would still have been rich and famous, with the ability to use my money and influence to contribute to causes I cared deeply about. like the Special Olympics and the After-School All-Stars program.

You might argue there was my reputation that I could have lost if any of those things I pursued had gone horribly wrong. But that assumes I cared what anyone thought about the goals I wanted to achieve with my life. It assumes that I wanted or needed the approval of some group of people to go after my dreams. The only approval I ever sought was from the judges at bodybuilding competitions, moviegoers at the box office, and voters at the ballot box. And if I didn't get it, if I lost or failed, I didn't complain. Instead, I used it as a learning experience. I went back to the gym or to the drawing board or to the briefing books, and I did the work to get better and smarter and to come back stronger the next time.

Where's the risk in that? The worst thing that can happen when you do the work to overcome adversity instead of quit in the face of it is that you fail again and learn one more way that doesn't work. Then that just forces you to switch gears, which gets you one step closer to your goal, because now you're more likely to be heading in the right direction.

Really, what do you have to lose?

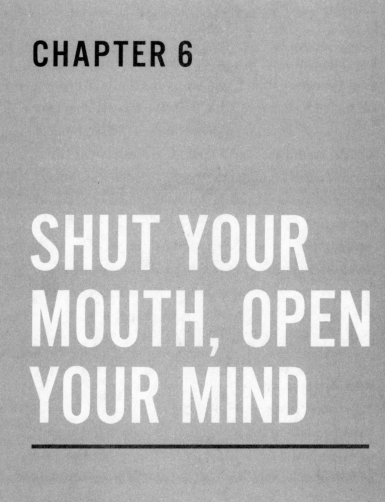

# CHAPTER 6

# SHUT YOUR MOUTH, OPEN YOUR MIND

The first adult I told about my vision for becoming a champion bodybuilder who took me seriously and supported my dream was a man named Fredi Gerstl. Fredi was the father of my friend Karl, who I trained with at the gymnasium in Graz as a young teenager. Fredi's story is an amazing one. He was Jewish but pretended to be Catholic during World War II to evade the Nazis, and then he joined the Resistance to help bring them down. After the war, he returned to Graz and took an interest in local business, local politics, and especially the local young people. With his wife, he opened a couple of cigarette and magazine kiosks, called *tabakladen,* on prime real estate at the train station and in the main square. They were perfectly situated for him to keep his finger on the pulse of life in Graz and the surrounding area, which would eventually help propel his political career as far as the presidency of Austria's upper house of Parliament. I met Fredi in the early 1960s, when he organized a group of us boys for athletic training and outdoor physical activities that taught us how to be tough and self-sufficient, but that also bonded us like Roman gladiators camped together out in the field preparing for battle. It was great fun, but there was also a catch. As Fredi told a reporter from the *Los Angeles Times* during my campaign for governor in 2003, "I gathered the young people together for sports, but the condition was they had to listen."

Listen to what? To whatever Fredi was interested in and thought was important for us to know, which was a lot. He didn't lecture us like a teacher. There were no quizzes at the end of the week. He was just planting seeds. "You might not understand this now," he would say of some idea that went over most of our heads, "but one day you will and you will be glad you know it." I didn't know the term for it then, but Fredi was a Renaissance man. He loved sports, dogs, opera, philosophy, and history, in addition to business and politics and countless other things, as I would learn over our fifty-year friendship. But it was his interest in learning and his focus on being open to new things—which I believe is the hallmark of a Renaissance man—that had the biggest impact on my life and I'm sure a lot of the other boys' lives as well.

Fredi became a father figure to us in a way our own fathers weren't capable of being, because he had vision in a way they didn't. In my case, because I was significantly bigger than the other boys my age, Fredi could see that being a serious bodybuilder had the potential to open doors for me, while my father thought the doors to future employers would be slammed in my face because bodybuilding wasn't serious. Fredi was younger than all our fathers, and he'd been on the right side of the war, which I think made it easier to keep an open mind about things as he got older, because he wasn't consumed by regret or shame like many of our fathers were. When you've fought for something you believe in and you've triumphed—when you've helped to literally save the world—I imagine it's easier to see the joy and possibility in new and beautiful things.

From the very beginning, Fredi told all of us boys that training our minds was just as important as training our bodies. He taught us that we can't just be hungry for success and money and fame and muscles. We have to be hungry for knowledge as well. Being in good shape with a strong, muscular physique will help you live a long, healthy life; it will help you get girls; it will allow you to do lots of difficult work to take care of your family; and for me it was of course necessary to become a bodybuilding champion. But if we wanted to be successful in *anything* we chose to do, at any point in our lives, young or old, and if we wanted to maximize our potential and our opportunities, then we needed to have a good head on our shoulders and an active mind.

Fredi made us see that the world was the ultimate classroom, and that we needed to be like a sponge, soaking up as much of it as we could. He made us understand that the way to become the kind of sponge that absorbs only the most useful knowledge was to always be curious. To listen and look more than we talked. And when we did talk, it was better to ask good questions than to make smart statements. And we needed to appreciate that all the information we absorbed, from whatever the source, could be put to use at any time, in service of any number of opportunities or problems or challenges, maybe tomorrow, maybe twenty years from now. There was no way to know for sure. But we could be certain that knowledge is power, and information makes you useful.

# THE WORLD CAN BE YOUR CLASSROOM

As a father, a businessman, and a public servant, nothing makes me crazier than the system in America that tries to push every kid into a four-year university. Of course, colleges are important. A college degree is a good thing. But it has its place. If you want to be a doctor or an engineer or an accountant or an architect, a university is the right place for you. There are jobs in this world that require a college degree and the studying that comes with it. It makes sense. We don't want hospitals filled with doctors who've never studied chemistry or commercial airliners that fly six million people every day to be designed by people who've never seen the inside of a math class.

But what if you're not sure what you want to do with your life? Or if you're sure that, whatever it is you'll want to do, it's not going to be something that requires a college degree? Does it really make sense to saddle yourself or your family with $250,000 in student loan debt? For what? A piece of paper? That is what the college experience for many young people has become. Ask them why they're going to college and they'll tell you it's to get a degree. That's like saying the reason you go to work is to get to the weekend. What about all the stuff in between? What about the purpose?!

This is the missing piece of the equation. Purpose. Vision. We aren't giving young people the time and space to discover a purpose or to create a vision for themselves. We aren't allowing the world to show them what is possible for their lives. Instead, right at the point where they have the least to lose and the most to gain from spending time out in the world, we're plucking them out of it and sticking them in four-year universities, which are the exact opposite of the real world.

I am living proof that the classroom where young people are likely to learn the most is out in the world. I learned about selling as an apprentice on the floor of a hardware store as part of vocational training. I learned how to think about big questions while sitting around Fredi's living room. Every other important thing I learned and carried with me into the rest of my life I either learned in the gym or I practiced and perfected there between the ages of sixteen and twenty-five. Goal setting, planning, working hard, pushing through failure, communicating, the value of helping others—for all of these things the gym was my laboratory. It was my high school, my college, and my graduate school all in one. When I finally stepped foot into an actual college classroom—and I took many college classes in the 1970s—it was with a purpose, in service of my vision. And I succeeded in those classes because I approached them the same way I learned to attack my bodybuilding goals. Like I said, for me all roads lead back to the gym.

And yes, we're talking about me here. I'm a crazy person with this stuff, we've already been over that. But when I walk the floor of the Arnold Sports Festival in Columbus, Ohio, every March, I see tens of thousands of people with similar stories. Men and women from all over the world who found their way to fitness and then found their way to a successful life *through* fitness. I'm talking about gym owners, firefighters, strongmen, and entrepreneurs selling fitness apparel, nutritional supplements, recovery drinks, physical therapy equipment, and so on. Most of these people aren't college graduates. And many of the ones who are will tell you that they don't actually use much of what they learned in college in their day-to-day business.

Parents, teachers, politicians, community leaders—

anyone who has the ear of young people needs to realize that there are millions of people out there who have created a vision for themselves and built happy, successful lives outside the university system. They are the plumbers and electricians and furniture refinishers and carpet cleaners we call when we have a problem that we don't know how to fix ourselves. They're general contractors, real estate agents, photographers. They're professionals in trades that they learned by doing, in real time, out in the real world. More than that, they are the glue that holds the economy together.

We should be pointing this out to our young people. We should be telling them that they can build their dream life with a hammer and nails, with a comb and scissors, with a saw and some sandpaper. And we should be doing this not just for their benefit but in our own self-interest. In countries all around the globe, we don't have enough people doing these jobs I'm describing. In the UK and the eurozone, lack of skilled labor has crippled the supply chain in some areas. In the United States, where political leaders are trying to bring computer chip manufacturing back into the country, there aren't enough skilled workers to build the buildings the manufacturing equipment is meant to go in. This isn't a new problem either. It's why when I was governor, I made huge investments in vocational and career education. Not only to support tradespeople, but to make people understand that what they do is critically important, and that we need to inspire more young people to go into those fields.

I don't think anyone fully understands why we have found ourselves in this situation, but I believe a big part of it is that we have been blinded by status, and it has made us closed-minded as a culture. It's why we value the number of degrees someone has over the number of happy customers they've served. It's why we love stories about entrepreneurship, but somehow if you work with your hands and own your own business, we don't call you an entrepreneur, we call you a small-business owner. And the irony is, if you compare a "small-business owner" with the kind of tech entrepreneur we lionize today (some of whose inventions are tearing us apart, by the way), the person who works with their hands is likely to be happier and to have owned their home before the highly educated entrepreneur ever made their first student loan payments. Even the dropouts we celebrate the most in our culture, like Bill Gates and Mark Zuckerberg, dropped out of Harvard, not high school or some state school that you've never heard of.

Well, let me tell you about a different kind of dropout. Her name is Mary Shenouda. She lives just down the hill from me in Venice. Mary is a high-performance private chef for professional athletes, actors, entrepreneurs, and executives who are at the top of their field and have to be at the top of their game at all times, which means she has to be at the top of her game too. A game she learned to play on her own. As a chef, as a performance specialist, Mary is entirely self-taught.

Mary has been teaching herself everything she knows since she dropped out of high school in the eleventh grade. Instead of going anywhere near college, Mary found her way into technology sales and, like I did at the hardware store in Graz when I was her age, learned how to sell her ass off. She was really good at it too. Sales was the first thing other than tennis that she found she was really good at, so she dove into that as a possible career.

A few years later, however, her focus started to shift toward cooking. It had to. Mary had been painfully sick for a long time, basically through her entire teen years, which was one of the reasons she dropped out of high school. It was only when she was in her early twenties that she discovered she was highly lactose intolerant, soy intolerant, and gluten intolerant. The typical food options available in restaurants and grocery stores were attacking her immune system and producing massive amounts of inflammation. If she ever wanted to feel good in her own body and eat any of her favorite dishes again, she was going to have to figure out a whole new way to make them that agreed with her system.

So she did. She became incredibly passionate about it in the process. She turned herself into an expert cook in less time than it takes a typical person to go through culinary school. And it just so happened that, at that very moment, the world around her was also going through the paleo diet revolution, as well as the keto revolution and the gluten-free revolution. More and more people were also replacing the dairy in their coffee or their ice cream with almond milk or coconut milk (now it's oat milk). These were the dietary areas that Mary found herself exploring as she came up with nutritious and delicious meals for herself.

It wasn't long before Mary realized that she was surrounded by a real business opportunity. Having grown up in Silicon Valley and living at the time in the San Francisco Bay Area, she was also surrounded by people who, had they been in her shoes, would have immediately applied to business school. But being a high school dropout, that path was not so readily available to her the way it would have been to others. And even if it was, being a seasoned salesperson by this point, with an idea she knew was good and a market she knew was growing, the world was telling her that the time was now to seize this opportunity. So she listened.

Mary started calling herself the "Paleo Chef," and she learned everything she could about turning this purpose-driven passion of hers into a business. She read books and taught herself how to read medical journal articles. She talked to old bosses and experts in all the fields she needed to understand. She picked the brains of clients and customers. She watched how other people who had no money, like her, built their businesses from the ground up. She made time for and listened to anyone who was willing to help her.

That was back in 2012. She has since built her private chef service, as well as a performance food product called Phat Fudge that she developed in conjunction with it, not just into successful businesses that make people better (her clients include NBA champions and Oscar winners) but into a lifestyle that gives her flexibility and control of her own destiny. She turned her vision into her reality.

All of this, from a high school dropout with an open mind and a killer work ethic.

For the record, I don't recommend dropping out of high school. You never know what might knock you out of commission or make pursuing your vision impossible, which could force you onto another, more traditional path for a while. In cases like that, having a high school diploma is kind of like having a driver's license. It doesn't make you better equipped, it just lets everybody else know that you're in the system and you know how to function within it.

That being said, the world is set up for you to do what Mary did with almost anything you are good at or any problem you are interested in solving, all without having to even think about college if you don't want to. It doesn't matter whether it's gluten-, soy-, and lactose-free food you want to create, whether it's becoming a fitness professional, or a landscaper, or turning your hobby into a side business after you retire.

I know it might sound like I'm picking on college, but that's only because the easiest way to close a person's mind is to make them feel like they can't afford to dream, and that's exactly what college has been doing to a lot of people. If you can avoid that happening to you, if you can listen to the world around you and pay attention to what gets you excited every morning, you will see that it's not all that difficult to find a passion or a purpose to build a vision around.

# BE CURIOUS

I have always been more like my character Julius in *Twins* than I have been like John Matrix in *Commando*. I'm not some kind of supersoldier who always knows what to do and is one step ahead of everyone; I'm an earnest person who is maybe a little naive about a few things that others take for granted, but who is mostly just curious to learn about the world.

As an immigrant, like I bet many of you are, and as someone who has transitioned between multiple careers, like many of you have, curiosity has been a superpower for me. It's magnetic. Simply by opening my mind to the wonders of the world around me, my curiosity has attracted many amazing opportunities to me. It has also attracted countless good, smart people into my life. The kind who like to teach and support and lift up others. This includes some truly remarkable figures who I've met over time, many of whom I'm honored to consider friends. People like Reg Park in the very beginning, then Muhammad Ali, Nelson Mandela, Mikhail Gorbachev, even the Dalai Lama and two different popes. My friends like to call me Forrest Gump because I've met every American president since Lyndon Johnson. Unlike Forrest, I didn't find myself in the same room as these great historical figures by accident; I met them because I was famous. But I got to know them and develop relationships with them because I was curious. I asked them questions about themselves and their experiences. I asked for advice. And then I listened.

Important, interesting, powerful people are drawn to those who ask good questions and listen well. When you're curious and you're humble enough to admit that you don't know everything, people like that *want* to talk to you. They want to help you. Your curiosity and humility show them you don't have too much of an ego to listen to them. When you're closed-minded, they know there's no reason to waste their breath. What's the point of trying to teach you something if you're already so sure you've got it all figured out?

Having the patience and humility to listen well is an essential ingredient of curiosity, and it's the secret to learning. Some of history's wisest thinkers and philosophers have been preaching to us about this for thousands of years, with lines like "We have two ears and one mouth so that we can listen twice as much as we speak." You see that idea pop up time and again throughout history. In the Bible: "Let every man be swift to hear, slow to speak." In the words of the Dalai Lama: "When you talk, you are only repeating what you already know. But if you listen, you may learn something new." Ernest Hemingway said, "When people talk, listen completely. Most people never listen." The late justice Ruth Bader Ginsburg said, "I'm a very strong believer in listening and learning from others."

These are all just different ways of saying that you don't know as much as you think you do, so shut your mouth and open your mind. I learned this lesson in a major way with *The Terminator*, which I easily could have lost if I'd let my agents and my ego argue with a guy who would become one of the greatest directors of all time.

I met Jim Cameron for the first time in the spring of 1983 over lunch at a restaurant in Hollywood, to talk about his script for *The Terminator*, which had been given to me by a guy named Mike Medavoy, who was the head of the studio that would eventually produce the movie. I was getting ready to start filming the sequel to *Conan the Barbarian*, and Mike, my agents, and I all believed that this could be my next movie, and that I should play Kyle Reese, the hero of the story.

It made sense on paper: Kyle Reese was a soldier from the future sent to save Sarah Connor and, by extension, the entire human race from a technologically advanced killing machine. It doesn't get more heroic than that. In our lunch meeting, however, we spent almost the entire time talking about the Terminator itself. It was definitely the character I found most fascinating and that piqued my interest the most. Reading the script, I had lots of questions and a few ideas about how someone should play a robot that is designed to look like a human being. I fired them all at Jim over the course of lunch. I could sense from his reaction to me that the breadth of curiosity my questions displayed and the depth of interest my ideas came from were surprising to him. I think he was expecting to meet with a meathead. He agreed that the Terminator was the most important character to get right. We even agreed about some of the specific things the actor who played the Terminator would need to do in order to embody the fact that he was a machine.

At some point during lunch, Jim became convinced I should be the Terminator. Or at least he was convinced that I *could be* the Terminator. In my head I thought I could be, too, but still, that was not the role I wanted to play and I told him that. I was Conan. Conan was a hero. I was meant to play heroes. My goal was to be the next great action hero. You don't get there by playing villains. Jim listened intently as I explained my position, which he understood. It was just the conventional Hollywood wisdom that I was describing.

Then it was my turn to listen. Jim's point was that this was not going to be a conventional Hollywood action film. There was time travel in this story. There was futuristic technology. It was science fiction. The rules are different in sci-fi. Plus, the Terminator wasn't the villain. The villain was whoever sent the Terminator from the future. The Terminator just ... is. We can make the character whatever we want based on how I decide to play it and he decides to shoot it, Jim said. That is, if I chose to take the role.

The more I thought about the project that night, the harder it was to get the image of me as the Terminator out of my head. All I could think about was my conversation with Jim. His words echoed in my ears. Jim had only made one movie before this, but his script was so original, and he really seemed to know what he wanted to do with it, that I couldn't help but be swayed by everything he said as he made the argument for me playing that role instead of Kyle Reese. Plus, I'd only starred in one movie myself by this point. Who was I to say that I knew better?

I called Jim the next day and told him I was in.

My agents were against the move. They held strong to the conventional wisdom against heroes playing villains. I heard them, but I didn't listen to them. Instead, I listened to my gut and followed where my curiosity led me. More importantly, I kept an open mind and listened to Jim. I really listened to him. And it produced the most consequential choice of my career. Not because *The Terminator* was successful, though that was good for my bank account. Listening to Jim talk about the Terminator in meetings, listening to how he directed me in rehearsals and on set, then watching how he edited my scenes, confirmed for me that I could be more than an action hero. I could be a *movie* star. A leading man.

The first big vision I had for my life emerged from watching Reg Park on the big screen in Graz in 1961. It evolved in a major way while listening to Jim Cameron over lunch in Venice in 1983, and it guided my choices for the next two decades. Hemingway was right. When people talk, you should listen to them.

## BE A SPONGE

Being curious and being a good listener are a big part of how to effectively utilize your relationships with other people in pursuit of your goals. I don't mean that in a manipulative way, only practically. When it comes down to it, people are resources. But it's only when you learn to soak up what those people tell you—not just let it go in one ear, out the other—that you truly begin to make yourself useful to others and become a resource yourself.

When I ran for governor, people who knew me said that I was going to love campaigning but hate sitting in the governor's office going over policy, because I always want action, action, action. People who didn't know me felt the same way, but for a slightly different reason. They thought I always wanted attention, attention, attention. Both perspectives were fair, to a degree, but they were also wrong. They failed to account for the fact that the governorship was the greatest classroom in the world, and they didn't fully appreciate that I have been a sponge of knowledge and new information my whole life, going all the way back to my younger days learning from Fredi and from other bodybuilders.

In the gym, if I saw someone trying a new training technique that didn't make sense to me, I didn't call them a forehead (my friend Bill Drake called everyone a "forehead," implying they had a low forehead like a Neanderthal). I asked the person about it because maybe it could help me. When I saw the great Vince Gironda do the side-lying triceps extension at his gym in North Hollywood back in the day, for instance, I admit I thought it looked a little Mickey Mouse with the tiny dumbbell he was using. But instead of knocking it because it looked girly or dismissing it entirely because Vince didn't come from a heavy lifting background, I tried it. I did forty sets during my next arms workout, which I had learned was the best way to see how a new movement impacts my body, and my outside triceps shook the whole next day. The exercise was so effective, I had to ask Vince about it.

*How did you come up with this exercise? Why does this work better than other similar movements? How should I best incorporate it into a workout?*

My questions served multiple purposes. The answers,

if they made sense to me, would alleviate any of my doubts or concerns. By being curious, like we just talked about, I showed humility and made myself an ally to Vince, which made it more likely that he might share other valuable training techniques. But most important of all, asking good "how" and "why" questions about something you're interested in increases the chances of that information sticking in your brain and connecting with other related bits of information—making all of it more useful to you when it's time for you to put it all to work in service of others.

That's why I loved being governor more than any job I'd ever had. It was an opportunity to soak up all this information about the way our society runs while being in a position to use that information to help millions of people. One minute, I was learning that we needed more prison guards because they were doing so much overtime that their working conditions were becoming less safe, and they were becoming chronically tired, which made them prone to errors and slipups in security protocols. The next minute, I was learning about prescription drug prices and health insurance premiums, or I was sitting with the smartest scientific minds in the world learning that millions of people die every year from pollution. A day later, I could be meeting with a team of civil engineers who explained how the state's thirteen thousand miles of levees were crumbling. I didn't even know we had that many miles of levees—more than Holland or Louisiana. Then, once my meeting with the engineers was over, it might be time to meet with a group of nurses who wanted to explain why California hospitals needed a better nurse-to-patient ratio than one to six. With one nurse for every six patients it becomes next to impossible for nurses to do all their work on a given shift. For instance, the average nurse can't lift a typical adult male on their own, so when that patient has to get up out of their hospital bed and go to the bathroom—a situation I experienced firsthand after my heart surgery in 2018—it sometimes takes two additional nurses, who are being pulled away from the work they have to do for their other patients. All of this I learned from a single conversation with a group of nurses!

I loved it. I was learning nonstop. The more I learned, and the more questions I asked of the people who were teaching me, the more I understood how things were connected and the better leader I became. Every day in Sacramento I felt like I was being given puzzle pieces to assemble a picture of how different systems worked, like a mental blueprint. And whenever the picture of one of those systems didn't make sense to me, or the blueprint looked broken, that's how I knew it was time for us to do something.

I was lucky. As governor, even if I wasn't naturally curious, I could make people explain things about the way the state worked until it made sense to me, no matter how long it took. Most people aren't so lucky. They don't have the power to make others explain the world to them, or they don't have mentors like Fredi Gerstl to show them how to open their minds and soak up the world like a sponge. They have to try to figure it out for themselves, which can be very intimidating and very discouraging without support.

This, I believe, is one of the reasons so many people feel stuck in their lives. They live in a world they don't understand. The world is what it is, and they are who they are, and it's just something they have to accept and deal with. It's their lot in life. Maybe they were born into a life in which others were rich and they were poor, or others were tall or smart or physically gifted and they were the opposite of those things—and no one explained to them that while there are some circumstances you can't change, there are others that you can change by being curious and by being a sponge and then using the knowledge you gain to craft a vision for yourself.

There is a famous line in *The Terminator*: "There's no fate but what we make for ourselves." No one has shown these poor souls that they can make their own fate. That they can change their circumstances so dramatically that it will make the unchangeable things irrelevant. Anyone can do this, in fact. Anyone can make their own fate. You can do it, starting at this very moment. By picking up this book, maybe you already have. If so, that's fantastic. Now I want you to reach out to someone in your life who maybe hasn't started working to change their circumstances because they don't think they can. It's important that we reach those people, because curiosity is the first thing that dies within someone who was raised to think the world is what it is and there's nothing they can do about it. After curiosity dies, the sponge that is their mind turns into a brittle brick that struggles to absorb anything new and becomes incredibly fragile when confronted with difficult decisions.

Do for them what Fredi Gerstl did for me, and what I, with this book, am trying to do for you. The world needs more sponges. It needs more smart, hopeful, driven, useful people with vision. It needs people who can dream up the world of tomorrow, which only happens when people are first able to soak up the knowledge of the world from today.

# PUT YOUR KNOWLEDGE TO GOOD USE

Use it or lose it. These words apply to so many areas of life, they should be considered a law of the universe.

In the gym, if you don't use a muscle, it shrivels up and dies. Something called atrophy.

In Hollywood, if you don't use your fame to do big projects or make a big impact, your star will fade and your chance to do either will fade along with it.

In government, if you have money earmarked for something in your annual budget and you don't use it that year, it will go away the next year and you will never see it again.

Use it or lose it is the rule with ripe fruit, political goodwill, media attention, coupons, economic opportunity, space to pass on the highway, all sorts of things. But most importantly, it's true of the knowledge you soak up over your lifetime. If you don't regularly flex your mind like a muscle and put your knowledge to work, it will eventually lose its power.

One of the first times I personally experienced the impact you can have by putting your knowledge to work was in the middle of my three years as chairman of the President's Council for Physical Fitness and Sports, from 1990 to 1993. As part of my duties working directly under President Bush, I visited schools in all fifty states. I met with local leaders to talk about policy. I gave speeches at schools to motivate kids and convince their parents to turn off the TV and go outside. I led roundtables and panel discussions with educators, medical experts, fitness professionals, health-care leaders, nutritional experts, and anyone else I thought could help us in our fight against childhood obesity and in support of physical education programs, which were being cut by states struggling with budget shortfalls. I did a lot of talking on these trips, but I spent most of my time as a sponge, watching and listening and asking questions, trying to learn from the people on the ground what was going on in their states. What issues were they facing? What things had they tried to save their physical education programs? What had worked? What had failed? What did they need? And why?

I left every event with my brain full of information, and for a while at least I had nowhere to put it other than into reports and recommendations that the council would generate each year. Then in 1992 I met a wonderful man named Danny Hernandez, who ran a program called the Inner-City Games (ICG) out of the Hollenbeck Youth Center in East Los Angeles, just fifteen miles across town from my home.

Danny was born and raised in a tough part of East LA called Boyle Heights. He graduated from high school there, he returned there to go to college after decorated military service in Vietnam, and he lives there to this day. He is like the eyes and the ears and the heartbeat of Boyle Heights. And over the years, he had come to notice that summertime, when school wasn't in session, was the time when the kids from his neighborhood were most vulnerable to drugs and gang violence, because they didn't have somewhere to go or something constructive to do every day. So in 1991, he started the ICG—an Olympics-style athletic and academic competition—for the kids in East LA as a way to get them off the streets.

Danny and I were introduced in the wake of the Los Angeles riots. The acquittal of four Los Angeles police officers that spring for the roadside beating of Rodney King a year earlier had exploded racial tensions in the city. Protests against the verdict led to a week of widespread looting, fires, violence, and property destruction, mostly in poorer neighborhoods like the one Danny served. Stores, apartment buildings, strip malls, and in some cases entire blocks went up in flames. Danny could sense that the summer, which was barely a month away, was going to be a crucial one for the kids, not just in Boyle Heights but all across Los Angeles. Things could go bad very quickly for everyone if community leaders weren't paying attention, if they didn't have their ear to the ground so to speak, as a half million kids between the ages of five and eighteen spilled out of classrooms and into the city streets. Danny's idea was to expand the ICG beyond East LA to include kids from the entire city, and he was looking for help from political leaders and high-profile people in town to raise awareness and money for the Inner-City Games.

That's when I came into the picture. Danny gave me a tour of the Hollenbeck Youth Center. It had a gym and a boxing ring and lots of sports equipment. There was a locker room with showers. It had quiet spots to do homework and adult mentors around for support. It even had a computer room with multiple machines, which was unbelievable for 1992. Except for the computers, the place reminded me of the gymnasium in Graz—it was a sanctuary full of possibility.

I soaked it all in as Danny talked to me about the work he'd been doing for the last decade, and I asked a lot of questions about what he hoped to do with the Inner-City Games. I believed that the more I knew, the better able I would be to help, and I really wanted to understand this place and Danny's mission.

I especially wanted to understand why there were no other programs like his. I'd been to schools in nearly every state by this point, and I hadn't seen or heard of a single program anywhere like the Inner-City Games. State and federal funds had always been really hard for Danny to secure, he told me, so that was probably why. It was also why he was talking to me about his program and not the mayor or the governor.

Danny was so impressive. His ambition for the center and the Games reminded me a lot of my early ambitions in bodybuilding and in Hollywood. We both had dreams that a lot of people probably thought were pretty crazy, but if you could see what we could see and you knew how much work we were willing to put in to make those dreams a reality, then you would realize they weren't so crazy after all.

I'd heard enough. I agreed to sign on. I joined as the Games Executive Commissioner to help Danny expand the ICG to Greater Los Angeles. Very quickly we formed the Inner-City Games Foundation as a nonprofit organization, and I spent the rest of the summer educating friends and Hollywood bigwigs and soliciting donations from them, while Danny secured corporate sponsorships. We weren't able to run the Games in time for summer break—the city was still recovering from the riots—but later that fall, the ICG hosted one hundred thousand local kids at multiple venues around Los Angeles as they competed in more than a dozen different athletic events, as well as essay and dance and art contests, where they could earn scholarships. In addition, there was a free career expo and free health-and-fitness screenings for kids and their families.

It was a huge success. Our efforts got a lot of attention, which is exactly what you need when you're trying to sell a vision like this to a city as big as Los Angeles. The Games in '92 also got national media exposure, which was even better, because it allowed Danny and me to fill the ICG bucket much the way I had in the past for the sport of body-building and for my movies. We were able to spread the message of the ICG on our terms, which had the effect of drawing in community organizers from other cities, like Atlanta and Chicago, who'd heard about what Danny had done the year before and wanted to see it for themselves, to see if it could work for their cities.

Whether or not the ICG could work for those cities wasn't a question that I was equipped to answer. What I did know for certain after my years as fitness czar is that each of those cities, and dozens more, *needed* a program like this because they had the same issue Los Angeles was dealing with: every summer, hundreds of thousands of kids had nowhere to be and no one watching after them.

But I also knew something else. This wasn't just a summer problem that cities were facing. This was a daily after-school problem as well. I'd begun seeing and hearing about it on my tour of America's schools. At the end of a school day, I would notice that some kids got picked up by parents, and others piled onto buses, but a lot of kids didn't do either. They hung around and goofed off or they left in small groups headed who knows where. I saw this pattern repeat over and over again, especially at middle schools, which don't have the same kind of extracurricular sports as high schools have. I was curious whether there was an explanation for this, so I asked the teachers and principals about what I was seeing. They said that as many as 70 percent of their students had parents who either weren't around or who worked but couldn't afford childcare, so the kids were home alone after school, which meant they were basically unsupervised until their parents got home from work. I also learned from the police chiefs in those cities that they referred to the time between the end of the school day and the end of the work day—approximately 3:00 to 6:00 p.m.—as "the danger zone," when kids were most susceptible to drugs and alcohol, to gangs and crime, and to teen pregnancy.

With the success of the Inner-City Games in the fall of 1992 and then again in the summer of 1993, I saw an opportunity to help Danny Hernandez grow the ICG beyond Los Angeles and to take it nationwide. My hope was that eventually, with enough support and funding, we could expand its mission beyond the Games in the summer to include a year-round after-school program. I had more than hope, though. I had a vision for this, and I believed I had the knowledge and capability to make it real.

This was a mission where I could finally take advantage of all the name recognition I'd developed over the previous two decades. I could utilize all the relationships I'd developed during that time. I could call every politician, government official, and subject-matter expert I'd met during my tour of all fifty states as fitness czar. I could leverage every bit of information I had learned from the panels and roundtables and Q&As and town halls I'd attended, from Anchorage to Atlanta. Like the sponge Fredi Gerstl taught me to be, I'd soaked up so much valuable information, and now it was time to wring it all out for at-risk kids across the country.

I am a strike-while-the-iron-is-hot kind of guy, so together with a powerhouse of a woman named Bonnie Reiss, we spun up a lobbying and fundraising machine as quickly as we could, and we hit the road. We traveled to cities all over America that we thought could use a program like the Inner-City Games and the more robust version of it that we were planning to build out. On my own dime, using my own plane, we flew everywhere and lobbied every city and state official who would sit down with us. We listened to them describe the issues they faced, many of which were related to finding the money to support our program in their city or even in just one of their schools. Just as I had during my time on the President's Council, I absorbed all that information and incorporated it into my understanding of the larger problems we were trying to solve. Then, working with Bonnie and Danny, with philanthropists in our network, and with state and federal agencies, we brought all of our knowledge to bear in offering solutions to these cities through the ICG Foundation.

The end result was the steady growth of the ICG into nine chapters across the country over the next few years. At the same time, we began to grow into a year-round, schools-based program called After-School All-Stars, which currently serves nearly 100,000 kids every day, in more than 450 schools across 40 American cities. It's a program that I am deeply proud to still be involved with, because it's a shining example of what is possible when you shut your mouth and open your mind. When you listen and learn and approach a problem with genuine concern. When you hold nothing back and give everything you have to make your corner of the world a better place.

Curiosity. Hunger for information. Being open-minded. Putting your knowledge to good use.

This, it turns out, is a formula for anyone to create real, meaningful change in the world, whether it's personal, professional, or political. It's also how you create change in your circumstances and make space for a vision to grow and evolve, which is essential, since I know that you want to grow and evolve too.

# CHAPTER 7

# BREAK YOUR MIRRORS

have a rule. You can call me Schnitzel, you can call me Termie, you can call me Arnie, you can call me Schwarzie, but don't ever call me a self-made man.

When I was younger, and my written English comprehension skills weren't as good as they are now, it always confused me when people called me that. *Self-made man?* I knew it was a compliment, but I still thought, What were these people talking about? What about my parents? They literally made me. What about Joe Weider? He brought me to America and made my earliest dreams a reality. What about Steve Reeves and Reg Park? They made it possible for me to dream about going from bodybuilding to movies in a realistic way. What about John Milius? He made me Conan the Barbarian.

I was maybe being too literal about the meaning of "self-made," but I still never believed that I was a self-made man. I believed that I was an example of the American Dream coming true. I believed (and still believe) that anyone can do what I did. But I felt, if anything, that this made me the opposite of a self-made man. Let's just analyze this for a second. If I am an example of what is possible in America, how could it be possible for me to be self-made, since I needed America for any of the successes I experienced to be possible. I was indebted to the existence of an entire country before I picked up my first barbell!

As I got older and I understood more of the nuance and the history behind the idea of the self-made man, I understood that what people were really trying to do was to compliment me for being hardworking, disciplined, motivated, dedicated—all the things you need to be in order to achieve your goals. And they were right, of course. I was all those things. No one lifted the weights or spoke the lines or signed the bills for me. But that doesn't mean I was self-made. Who I am, where I am, why I am here, what I have had the opportunity to do—this is all because of the impact of hundreds of special people in my life.

I'm not alone in this. We are all here thanks to the contributions of other people. Even if you never had a positive influence in your life; even if everyone you've ever run into was an obstacle or an enemy or they did nothing but hurt you—they have all still taught you something. That you're a survivor. That you're better than that, better than them. They showed you what not to do and who not to be. You are here today, right now, reading this book trying to better yourself, because of the people in your life—for better and for worse.

None of us has ever done anything on our own when you really think about it. We have always had help or guidance. Others have paved or pointed the way for us in some form or another, whether we were aware of it beforehand or not. And now that *you* know this, it's important for you to recognize that you have a responsibility to give back. To help others. To send the ladder back down and lift the next group up. To pay it forward. To be useful.

And let me tell you something: when you fully embrace that responsibility, it will change your life and improve the lives of countless others. You will wonder why you hadn't realized this much earlier. What began as a responsibility will quickly become a duty, which will eventually feel like a privilege that you will never want to let go of and will never take for granted.

# EVERYONE BENEFITS FROM GIVING BACK

A book like this one is a conversation between two people, the author and the reader. You and me. It's not me talking to the whole world, it's me talking to you. It's a profound and sacred relationship, in my opinion. But something weird sometimes happens with books like this, where the goal of the author is to motivate you, the reader, to create a vision for your life, to think big, and to do whatever it takes to achieve that vision. These books can become permission slips for selfishness. They can be used to justify a "me against the world" kind of attitude that turns self-improvement into a zero-sum game. For you to get richer, someone has to get poorer. For you to get stronger, someone must become weaker. For you to win, everyone else has to lose.

Let me tell you, outside of direct athletic competition, it's almost all bullshit. Life isn't zero-sum. We can all grow together, get richer together, get stronger together. Everyone can win, in their own time, in their own way.

How that happens is by focusing on all the ways we can give back to the people in our lives, whether they're our family, our friends, our neighbors, our collaborators, or just our fellow humans who breathe the same air we do. How can we help them achieve their own visions? How can we support them in their goals? What can we do to help them get better at the things they love to do? What can we give to those in need? What you will discover as you answer each of these questions for yourself in your own relationships is that you will get back exactly what you give.

I felt this first, and most powerfully, in the gym with my training partners. We always pushed one another. We shared training techniques and nutritional tips. We supported one another with encouragement but also literally by spotting for one another as we lifted max weight or we lifted to failure. We all realized that we'd be competing against one another eventually, so it wasn't like we were unaware that each of us was helping our competition get better, but we also knew that if our training partners got stronger, that meant they could push us more, which meant we could get stronger.

Helping one another out like that didn't just benefit us as individual bodybuilders; it also helped the sport of bodybuilding. I was the face of international bodybuilding in the 1970s, but I would have been only a novelty, and bodybuilding would have seemed like nothing more than a circus sideshow, if I had been up onstage with a bunch of competitors who were orders of magnitude less muscular or defined than I was. And who knows if I would have gotten to the level I did. I don't know if I would have achieved the body I had for each of my Mr. Olympia titles if I hadn't had Franco Columbu pushing me as a training partner or if Frank Zane hadn't lived with me for a few months and showed me his tricks to get better definition. Bodybuilding reached the heights that it did because a whole group of us trained together in the same gyms and helped one another get better, which made the competitions better, which made the sport bigger.

I experienced this same positive feedback loop in movies. Hollywood is full of very insecure actors who, when they aren't given the right guidance or support by their inner circle, will turn a movie into a zero-sum game. They will try to dominate every scene they're in, to get more screen time than their costars, and to blow other actors off the screen. They think this is what great actors do. That this is how you become a star or win awards. The reality is, that kind of personal ambition and me-first behavior makes movies worse. It makes them awkward, and it affects the viewing experience in a negative way. But when actors help one another in their scenes, when they set one another up, when they make space for one another to have great moments and memorable performances, that's when movies go from good to great, and they connect more deeply with audiences. That's when they become successful. And having a successful movie means the actors who were in it are more likely to get offers for other, bigger movies that are more lucrative than the movie they just did together.

By being selfless, by helping your costar or your competitor or your colleague, you have the ability to make everybody's life better and to create a positive environment where you can thrive and find happiness as well. This is why we love TV shows with great ensemble casts. It's why we admire companies like Patagonia, which put customers and their employees ahead of profits. It's why we celebrate great sports teams like the 2017 Golden State Warriors or those amazing Spanish national soccer teams, because they are amazing passers of the ball who play a team game that gets everyone involved and makes everyone better.

On the flip side, this is also why we have such complicated feelings about selfish superstar athletes, egotistical CEOs, and narcissistic politicians. They almost never make other people better. Even when they're "on our team," we only put up with them as long as they're winning. The minute they start losing or things start going bad, we want to trade them, fire them, vote them out of office. Because at that point, what's the benefit of putting up with a selfish bastard who only thinks about themself?

But you don't have to be pursuing a goal or a big vision to experience the benefits of helping others. There is a lot of science that indicates the simple act of giving back significantly increases the happiness of the giver, and that the increase starts to happen almost immediately. In 2008, researchers at Harvard did an experiment where they gave one group of participants five dollars and another group twenty dollars and told them to either spend it on themselves or give it away. When the researchers followed up with participants at the end of the day, they found that the people who gave their money away reported having a much better day than those who kept their money.

And here's the really interesting part: there was no meaningful difference in the level of increased happiness between the people who gave away five dollars compared to those who gave away twenty. It's not as if the people who gave away twenty dollars experienced four times as much additional happiness. Which means it's not about the amount that you give, it's about the fact that you give at all. It's the act of giving that produces the increased happiness.

Think about that: You can make someone's day better and your own day better with the same act of kindness and generosity. And you don't need to be rich or flush with cash to do it.

## HOW TO GIVE BACK

It's easy for someone like me, with all my life experience and resources to call upon, to sit here and tell you how important it is to give back or how good it feels to help others. But I know that the benefits are not always so obvious when you're young and poor and still trying to figure out what you want your life to look like. I also know that it's not so simple when you're older and working multiple jobs, when you have lots of mouths to feed, or when every waking hour is consumed by worrying about your own problems.

It can feel like there's no time in your schedule for giving back. And when you do find time, your head has been down for so long trying to grind, or to provide, or to make your vision a reality, that it can be overwhelming to figure out how best to use that time, or whether your time is even valuable to somebody else.

You end up saying to yourself things like, "Who am I? I'm just a nobody trying to get by." Or "What can I do? I don't have any special skills." Or "What do I have to offer? I'm not rich and famous like these other people."

The first thing to realize is that at the simplest, most basic level, you don't have to rearrange your life to help other people. You just have to keep your eyes and ears open and be engaged with the world around you. When you see someone struggling—with a bag of groceries or a difficult emotion—stop and give them a hand or a hug. If a friend you haven't talked to for years calls in the middle of the night, answer the phone. If there is someone who looks like they might need help, answer the call, whether they asked for help or not. Lighten their burden, even if it's only for five minutes or fifty feet. Helping others is a simple practice that requires nothing more than awareness, willingness, and a little bit of effort. Without actively seeking it out, just by being connected to your environment, you will have opportunities every day to help someone else. And trust me when I tell you, it will make you feel great when you do.

The second thing to realize is that you have more to offer than you know. For instance, I know you have the time. If we looked at the full twenty-four-hour breakdown of your day, I guarantee you have an hour to spare at least once or twice a week. Do you speak a foreign language? Are you good at math? Do you know how to read? You could tutor middle-school kids once a week at an after-school program near your house. You could read to elementary school kids at the local library or to patients at the children's hospital. Do you have a reliable car or van? You could deliver meals to the elderly or drive residents at assisted living facilities to their physical therapy appointments. Are you handy? Do you own tools? You could help fix up the sports fields in your hometown before the season gets started.

It doesn't even have to get that complicated in terms of skills. Can you walk and afford a box of large garbage bags? The great American writer David Sedaris has been picking up litter along the roads near his house in the English countryside as part of his daily morning walks for so long that the county named a garbage truck after him and Queen Elizabeth once invited him to Buckingham Palace for tea.

Not that you should need a nice house to motivate you to pick up trash in your neighborhood. You don't need a house, period. In West Los Angeles, a homeless man named Todd Olin became a local legend for spending hours every day, *for years*, cleaning up the streets of his Westchester neighborhood. He picked up trash, picked weeds, cleaned graffiti, cleared drains and sewer grates. And he started with nothing but a couple of shopping carts and a cheap plastic trash picker.

Giving back isn't something that has to happen every day either. In 2020, a sixteen-year-old high school student from Tucson, Arizona, named Lily Messing started a group called 100+ Teens Who Care Tucson that gets together only four times a year. Each member of the organization, which is made up of high school students, commits $25 each quarter—so $100 total for the year—

then they identify a local organization that needs help, and they pool their money for that quarter and donate it directly to the organization. Since 2020, they've given more than $25,000 to groups that serve local children, animals, domestic-abuse victims, and the homeless. Twenty-five dollars, four times a year. That's all it took to have that kind of impact!

If you're still struggling to think up ways you can give back, don't focus on what you have or what you know, take a personal inventory of what others have done for you in your life and try to pay it forward by doing those same things for others who might be in a similar situation. If you had a great soccer coach when you were a kid, get involved in youth soccer. If you got a scholarship from a local service organization that helped you go to college, get in contact with that organization and see how you might be able to contribute to their scholarship fund for the current crop of high school seniors. As a way to pay forward Joe Weider's generosity in bringing me to America, one of the things I do is identify ambitious foreign citizens with big, worthy dreams and sponsor them for visas and green cards by writing letters on their behalf using my personalized stationery with the California governor's seal at the top of it. You don't have to be connected and you don't need to get creative in order to give back, you just need to give it a little thought.

Last chapter we talked a lot about how being curious, being a sponge, and asking good questions are tools for opening your mind to the possibilities of the world. Well, they are also tools for opening your heart to its problems, and to the ways you might be a part of their solution. Sometimes those problems are small and they only affect one person who just needs a little bit of help very quickly. Other times those problems can be massive or chronic or systemic, and helping to solve them becomes a cause you give back to, like it did for Lily Messing, or becomes part of your life's mission, like it did for Danny Hernandez and Mary Shenouda.

Of course, you can do both. I send a newsletter to hundreds of thousands of people every day to inspire them to be healthy and fit. It is, in many ways, a continuation and evolution of my work combating obesity in the early 1990s as fitness czar. At the same time, I get an equal amount of joy from randomly spending ten minutes with some old geezer in the gym to show him proper form for a pulldown, or talking to a seventeen-year-old kid who wants to start his own roofing business.

In either case, whether you've helped hundreds with your work or changed one life with your words of wisdom, you will have given back in the most profound way, because you will have changed the world. If you're still not sure what you have to offer, then just be present and stay focused on the little things. Little things always have a tendency to become big things, and I am confident that one day something small will lead you to something big that you feel equipped to give back to in a bigger way.

This is often how it happens for kids working toward becoming Eagle Scouts, the highest rank in the Boy Scouts program. The last step on the road to becoming an Eagle Scout is completing a service project that has a significant impact on the local community. Essentially, they have to design their own way of giving back. Most of these kids figure out what they want their service project to be in a short amount of time because they've had their eyes and ears open for years, engaged with their communities and ready to respond to those who have needed help.

Maybe they're always helping people lift shopping carts or baby carriages up onto the sidewalk because the curbs in their town are too high, so for their project they decide to pull permits, raise money from local businesses, and get a local contractor to help repair road surfaces and build handicap-accessible curb ramps all over town.

Maybe they're always helping neighbors look for their dogs who keep escaping from a park near their house because the fence around the park is old and has gaps in it. So they decide to redesign and rebuild the fencing with some of their fellow Scouts using donated materials from the local hardware store, and then they petition the city council to get the space officially designated as a dog park so that future maintenance is taken care of.

There are a thousand versions of this story from the Eagle Scouts, but the best part is that there are a million ways you can take the lesson at the heart of them to make use of your time, skills, and resources for the benefit of others. And in my experience, once you start, you don't stop.

# GIVING BACK BECOMES AN ADDICTION

My first experience with giving back in an organized way happened in the late 1970s, when I got an invitation to help train Special Olympics athletes in powerlifting at a university up in the northwest corner of Wisconsin. Over the course of two or three days, I worked with groups of teenage boys with different degrees of intellectual disabilities as part of a study to see if lifting weights could be safe for them as athletes and beneficial as a therapeutic tool. The entire experience was incredibly powerful, but it was our first day together, focused on the bench press, that sticks with me in vivid detail even now.

I remember the kids were a little cautious and withdrawn at first. I remember flexing and posing for them and letting them squeeze my biceps or poke my chest as a way to coax them out of their shells. I remember how good it felt to earn their trust and to watch their enthusiasm grow as, one by one, they lay down on the bench and positioned themselves under the bar to lift weights for the first time in their lives. I remember a few of them struggled. Seeing the bar directly above their heads and then feeling gravity press the weight down on them through their hands was a little scary. The sensation was probably as foreign to those kids as teaching and communicating with them was for me. But I remember thinking, if they had the courage and strength to face their fears and try something new, I couldn't allow my uncertainty to get in the way and potentially let them down. Instead, I tried to match their kindness and their enthusiasm and their openness. By the end of the day, I remember, each kid had done multiple sets on the bench press. Even the boys who were the most terrified got under the bar and knocked out some reps, including one boy who panicked initially and started screaming until I was able to calm him down by standing him next to me and making him my official rep counter.

I will never forget that boy. After helping me count off reps for some of the other boys, I could sense that he was starting to get more comfortable around the weights. He'd watched them lift the weight and seen that it hadn't crushed them. I asked him if he wanted to give it another shot, and he said yes. His friends were so excited for him. He lay down on the bench with his head between the vertical bar supports; I stood behind him, and I slowly placed the bar in his hands.

"Now give me ten reps," I said. He knocked them out like they were nothing. His friends went wild for him. A smile as wide as the barbell bloomed across his face. "I think you're ready for more weight," I said.

I added a ten-pound plate to each side. "Try to give me three reps," I said. His friends cheered him on. He took a deep breath and pushed them out with very little effort.

"Wow, you're so strong," I said. "I think I might have some competition pretty soon. Can you do more?"

He nodded excitedly. So two more ten-pound plates went on. And he did another three reps. Within the space of an hour and a half, this boy had gone from being completely terrified of the barbell to lifting eighty-five pounds three times with no assistance. He got up from the bench, I gave him a high-five, and his friends mobbed him.

Standing there watching these young boys celebrate the achievement of their friend, I was filled with a kind of joy that was almost spiritual. It was so overwhelming that I was confused. I hadn't made any money. This wasn't a move that advanced my career. Doing things like this wasn't really a part of my larger vision yet. And if I'm being honest, it didn't feel like I was doing all that much in terms of exertion or sacrifice. So why was I this happy?

I realized it was because I'd helped these kids. By doing something as simple as showing up, being supportive and encouraging, and teaching a couple of things, I'd changed this boy's life. He now had proof that he could do this, that he was strong enough not just to lift weights but to overcome his fears. I'd helped him learn something about himself that he could take with him into new and uncomfortable and scary situations for the rest of his life.

He was never going to be the same after this day. Neither were his friends. And neither was I.

It turns out that there had actually been a lot in this experience for me, just not in the sense I'd tended to measure things before. I was able to use my knowledge and my expertise to help this group of young people less advantaged than me get better at something, get stronger, get more confident, and feel better about themselves. I'd given back, and I'd done it for no other reason than because they needed help and someone had asked me.

Immediately, I wanted to do more of it. If you were in my shoes, you probably would have felt that way too. But don't take my word for it. Look at the science. In multiple studies over the last forty years, psychologists and neuroscientists have learned that giving back, whether through charitable donations or volunteering, releases oxytocin and endorphins. These are the same hormones your brain produces during sex and working out. Giving back is also known to produce a neurochemical called vasopressin, which is associated with love. In fact, just *thinking* about or remembering moments of being charitable triggers the release of these same hormones.

Social scientists have a name for this phenomenon: they call it "helper's high." That's how powerful giving back is. It's a natural feel-good drug with *highly* addictive properties. I know all this now, but in the months and years that followed my weekend up in Wisconsin, I was just hunting the oxytocin and the endorphin high like an addict chasing the dragon.

As a result of our work together, the university researchers and the officials from the Special Olympics found that weight lifting gave the kids more confidence than almost any other sport they did. The impact was so significant, they wanted my help developing a powerlifting competition for the Special Olympics Games and figuring out which lifts should be included as part of it. I jumped at the chance. We decided to start with the bench press and the deadlift, because they are the simplest movements and put the kids with balance issues or a motor coordination deficit at the least amount of risk. They're also the most fun to watch and be a part of because they involve the largest amount of weight being lifted. After helping to design the program, I worked with groups of kids in a number of other cities around the country and then signed on as an official International Trainer. Within a couple of years, powerlifting would be included at regional Special Olympics events in the United States and eventually become a staple of the International Games, where it remains one of the most popular sports with both athletes and spectators. To this day I love cheering on those strong men and women at every Special Olympic Games, and I'm incredibly proud that my daughter and son-in-law have joined the cause as global ambassadors.

Later, it was all my work with the Special Olympics that persuaded President Bush to ask me to chair the President's Council for Physical Fitness and Sports. At the time, I was as busy and as in demand as I'd ever been. I was filming two movies a year and doing all the international promotion that goes along with them. I was making $20 million per movie. But the joy I got from pumping up those kids at the Special Olympics was greater than any feeling I ever had walking a red carpet, and it was more valuable to me than another huge payday, so the chance to replicate that feeling by helping even more kids, including some of the country's most vulnerable schoolchildren, was a no-brainer. I said yes immediately and committed during my entire tenure to travel on my own dime, use my own plane, and to pay for everyone's food and lodging during our tour of all fifty states.

My growing roles with the Special Olympics and the President's Council took up a lot of free time, but not so much that it stopped me from looking for more and more ways to give back. I was hooked. I have no doubt that helper's high played a big part in getting Danny Hernandez and me in a room together that first time in 1992, for example. I know it was a big part of pushing to expand the Inner-City Games to other cities over the rest of the decade and to grow its mission into a national year-round after-school program.

This is just what happens when giving back gets its hooks into you. Like a drug, you don't just want to do more of it, you want to go bigger too. You want to help more people, more often, with more things. For me, that eventually took the form of giving up my big movie paychecks, running for governor of California and refusing the taxpayer-funded salary, and then, once my term was up, shifting my effort to the Schwarzenegger Institute at USC and the Schwarzenegger Climate Initiative, where our goals of reforming our political system to shift power from the politicians to the people and terminating pollution have the potential to help hundreds of millions, if not billions, of people.

Every day I wake up thinking about these things, and they fill me with an incredible sense of purpose. That same feeling is possible for you, for anyone, once you take that first step toward giving back and letting the endorphins flow through your veins.

## SHATTER THE GLASS

It's interesting to look back over the forty-plus years since I made that trip up to Wisconsin, and to see how my vision evolved as my priorities shifted. At first, I was 100 percent me-focused, and my vision was all about professional success and personal fame and fortune. That vision guided all my decisions, and the extent to which I was happy helping other people was defined mostly by how it fit into that vision. But as time went on, and giving back became a greater part of my life, the dial started to turn more we-focused. I was happy helping other people not because it advanced my personal goals, but because *it was my personal goal*. It was no longer a means to an end, it was an end in and of itself.

Making giving back a focal point of my life was cemented for me shortly after my time on the President's Council, during a speech by my late father-in-law, Sargent Shriver, to the graduating class at Yale University.

Sarge, as his friends called him, was kind, brilliant, and thoughtful. He led from the heart unlike anyone I have ever met. He cared deeply about people, and he put his money (and his time) where his mouth was.

Sarge founded the Peace Corps, Head Start, VISTA (Volunteers in Service to America), Job Corps, Upward Bound, and a number of other charitable organizations that helped underserved groups in America and around the world. He was also chairman of the board of the Special Olympics, which his wife, Eunice, my mother-in-law, founded in addition to her other work in support of people with intellectual disabilities. It's not an exaggeration to say that the Shrivers spent their entire adult lives in service to humanity.

At the time of his Yale Day speech, Sargent was in his late seventies. He'd seen the world and experienced a lot. He was full of wisdom that he wanted to share with the next generation of leaders about having the power to make the world into the place they wanted it to be. But he also had a piece of advice.

"Break your mirrors!" he said. "Yes indeed—shatter the glass. In our society that is so self-absorbed, begin to look less at yourself and more at each other. Learn more about the face of your neighbor and less about your own.

When you get to be thirty, forty, fifty, or even seventy years old, you'll get more happiness and contentment out of counting your friends than counting your dollars. You'll get more satisfaction from having improved your neighborhood, your town, your state, your country, and your fellow human beings than you'll ever get from your muscles, your figure, your automobile, your house, or your credit rating. You'll get more from being a peacemaker than a warrior. Break the mirrors."

Sargent gave that speech in 1994, nearly thirty years ago now. His message is still as relevant as ever, don't you think? I believe it will be just as relevant for many generations to come. I say this realizing that advice like Sargent's often seems to come from elites who like to talk about saving the world from going to shit while they relax in the comfort and safety of their yacht or their gated summer home.

"Easy for him to say," you might be thinking to yourself.

What you need to understand is that Sargent wasn't saying there is no value or happiness to be found in personal ambition. He appreciated that, while having muscles isn't the most important thing in the world, having a strong, healthy body is good for you and essential to a long life. He knew that having a nice car that drives well and you can rely on gives you one less thing to worry about. He recognized that having a big-enough house to fit your whole family and that feels like home can be a source of great pride.

Sargent's point was that giving back is a source of *greater* contentment, in part because it puts personal ambition in proper perspective. I would even go one step further—and I am the one speaking from experience now—to say that breaking your mirrors and taking care of all those people behind the glass who could use your help is not just a greater source of happiness, it actually makes those things you want for yourself more meaningful and more precious.

That all sounds very philosophical, I know, but I saw what it looked like in practice during the fire season when I was governor. At least once between June and October every year, I would find myself at the scene of a massive forest fire, visiting with firefighters as they rested between twelve- to eighteen-hour shifts battling fast-moving walls of flames in extreme heat and dangerous conditions in an effort to save homes and lives. I saw that they were exhausted from hiking in and out of valleys, from cutting down trees and digging firebreaks, and I would ask them questions about how they were feeling, and they would be as humble as their actions were heroic. But what was most remarkable to me was that on more than one occasion, I'd be talking to a local firefighter who was on the front line while their own house was potentially burning to the ground. Everything they owned, their prized possessions, the place where they were raising a family—all of it could have been on the verge of going up in flames at any moment, and these firefighters hadn't given a second's thought to whether or not their proper place was back trying to save their own homes or out there on the fire line trying to help their neighbors.

Forget about breaking their mirrors, these were the kind of people who never had mirrors to begin with. They were always looking out for others. Giving back and helping people is just what they did. They were 100 percent we-focused, and I have looked up to them as role models in selflessness and sacrifice because of that ever since. I think we all should. I don't think many of us can achieve that level of selflessness, but we can certainly aspire to it.

In my own case, I would say that today my life is *mostly* we-focused, and the main reason that any of it is me-focused is so that I can keep making money to support all the we-focused stuff I care about. The ability to so quickly send a million dollars to the First Responders Fund in March 2020, for example, was the result of continuing to spend time on personal ambitions and knowing that there will always be money there to give back and to help solve big, urgent problems that are being bungled by politicians who don't actually care about helping others.

I am not sharing these stories with you as a way to tell you to do what I did, or to do what firefighters and commandos and first responders do. I am also not asking you to be Robin Hood or Mother Teresa, or to abandon your personal ambition or your personal possessions. I am only asking you to break your mirrors and do for others what you are able to do. I am asking you to give back. To pay it forward. To be useful as often as you can. And I am asking you to do that for the same reason that any of us have chosen to give back. Because we owe a debt of gratitude to the people who got us where we are today. Because we can do for the next generation exactly what the previous generation did for us. Because it will make the world a better place. Because it will make you happier in ways you could never have anticipated.

One thing you learn when you've lived long enough and worked hard enough to see your wildest dreams come true, is that we're all connected. We're all in this thing called life together. It's not a zero-sum game. It's one that can have multiple winners. An unending amount of winners, really . . . as long as you make giving back part of the rules of the game. When we make giving back a part of life, when we break our mirrors so we can see all the people behind the glass who could use our help, that's when we all benefit.

It doesn't matter how young or old you are, how much or how little you have, how much you've done or how much you have left to do. In every case, giving more will get you more. Want to help yourself? Help others. Learn to start from that place, and that is how you will become the most useful version of yourself—to your family, to your friends, to your community, to your nation . . . and to the world.

# A FINAL THANK-YOU

When I read Marcus Aurelius's *Meditations,* I was struck by the fact that the first book in what is basically a two-thousand-year-old journal was nothing more than a list of people in Marcus's life who helped him or taught him something valuable. Talk about a powerful way to remind yourself that you aren't self-made.

As I worked my way through writing this book, and memories of the people at the center of all these stories I've just told came flooding back to me, I decided that instead of a traditional acknowledgments section, it would be more useful to end the book the way Marcus Aurelius began his.

Once you finish reading, you should make your own list. It will keep you humble. And when you need advice or help or inspiration, the list will be useful to refer back to as well.

I learned discipline and the importance of being useful, no matter what, from my father.

I learned about love and sacrifice from my mother.

Karl Gerstl and Kurt Marnul showed me how to lift. Harold Maurer trained me.

Steve Reeves and Reg Park paved the way for bodybuilders to become movie stars and gave me my blueprint. Clint Eastwood was a movie idol who later became a dear friend.

Fredi Gerstl opened my mind and honed my natural inquisitiveness into a skill for asking good questions.

Franco Columbu was my best friend and my confidant, my partner in crime for more than fifty years. He was also my training partner, and along with my other training partners like Dave Draper and Ed Corney, he pushed me to lift heavier, go further, and get bigger.

Albert Busek was the first of the muscle magazine writers to see the promise in me, declaring bodybuilding had entered a "Schwarzenegger Era" and taking some of the best and earliest photos of me—photos that got the attention of . . .

Joe Weider, who paid my way to America and gave me

a soft place to land. He was also a consummate salesman and a brilliant brand builder who I took a lot of pointers from.

Frank Zane and Sergio Oliva inspired me to find a new gear by kicking my ass. They also became friends who shared their training knowledge freely, even though we were competitors.

Olga Assad taught me how to invest in real estate.

In my movie career, Sylvester Stallone inspired me with his unbelievable talent and became the rival I needed to fuel my drive for my rise in Hollywood, and then he became a dear friend whom I can call about anything.

John Milius, Jim Cameron, and Ivan Reitman each took a chance on me in their own way and let me show them I was up to the challenge of being a mainstream movie star and a leading man.

Sargent and Eunice Shriver were my role models for giving back.

President George H. W. Bush mentored me and showed me how to turn my interest in paying back the debt I owed into real public service.

Nelson Mandela helped me fully understand the horrors of racism and prejudice, as well as the power of forgiveness.

Muhammad Ali showed me what real grit and perseverance looks like, and what it takes to really stick to your guns.

Mikhail Gorbachev opened my eyes to how the geopolitical system really works and why doing the right thing for the most people is so hard to do.

My old friend and mentor Jim Lorimer taught me so many things, they could be their own book. But I will never forget that he championed the Arnold Sports Festival with me, and his was the lone, unequivocal voice when I was thinking about running for governor that said, without question, that I should go for it, that I was ready. He gave me so much confidence.

All our After-School All-Stars and all the Special Olympics athletes I've watched and worked with have been living reminders that things in life might not always go the way you want them to in the beginning, but that isn't an excuse to stop trying or to stop striving or to not be grateful for the things you do have.

I've also been lucky to have the love of amazing women in my life. For decades, Maria stood by my side for every decision and, to this day, is such a fantastic mother to our children. For the last ten years, Heather has been my partner and confidante, there with me through ups and downs, adding to our menagerie of animals every year.

My kids, at every age, have humbled me when I needed it. They also inspired me to try my hardest to build a world that will be better long after I'm gone. So did California's voters, for that matter.

Lastly, but certainly not least, there is my team—the men and women who have assembled around me over the years and stayed with me through the many phases of my life, including those who have joined me more recently for projects like this book or my Netflix shows. You keep me on my toes, you help me shine, you make me smarter, and, most importantly, no matter how hard we work, we always laugh.

I could go on and on listing people who have helped me achieve my dreams and create the life I envisioned for myself beginning all those years ago back in my little village in Austria, but I think you get the point by now.